Economic Evaluation of Soviet Socialism

Soviet Socialism

(Pergamon Policy Studies-24)

Pergamon Titles of Related Interest

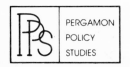

PERGAMON
POLICY
STUDIES

Economic Evaluation of Soviet Socialism

Alan Abouchar

Pergamon Press
NEW YORK • OXFORD • TORONTO • SYDNEY • FRANKFURT • PARIS

Pergamon Press Offices:

U.S.A.   Pergamon Press Inc., Maxwell House, Fairview Park,
                Elmsford, New York 10523, U.S.A.

U.K.   Pergamon Press Ltd., Headington Hill Hall,
                Oxford OX3 0BW, England

CANADA   Pergamon of Canada Ltd., 150 Consumers Road,
                Willowdale, Ontario M2J 1P9, Canada

AUSTRALIA   Pergamon Press (Aust) Pty. Ltd., P O Box 544,
                Potts Point, NSW 2011, Australia

FRANCE   Pergamon Press SARL, 24 rue des Ecoles,
                75240 Paris, Cedex 05, France

FEDERAL REPUBLIC   Pergamon Press GmbH, 6242 Kronberg/Taunus,
OF GERMANY   Pferdstrasse 1, Federal Republic of Germany

Library of Congress Cataloging in Publication Data

Abouchar, Alan.
  Economic evaluation of Soviet socialism.

  (Pergamon policy studies)
  Includes bibliographies and index.
  1. Russia—Economic conditions—1918-
I. Title.
HC335.A567 1979   330.9'47'085   79-845
ISBN 0-08-023870-X

Printed in the United States of America

J.A., A.J., and M.A.C.

Contents

CHAPTER

List of Figures and Tables

Preface

This book has grown out of my lectures on the Soviet economy given over a number of years at the University of Toronto. The lectures constitute an attempt to evaluate the economic achievements of Soviet socialism from different points of view, recognizing that an assessment of some aspects of performance may be positive from one point of view and negative from another. For example, existing income inequalities may be substantial and deplorable from the viewpoint of some Marxists' insistence on equality and on returning to the workers the fruits of their labor. However, the present situation does nevertheless represent a substantial achievement when compared to what might have been in the absence of the revolution, which is a more relevant question for a large part of the world's population today. Or again, the Soviet economy has not succeeded in eliminating inflation; but are the implications for the economy the same as in a capitalist developed or industrializing economy? Can anything like a "structuralist" justification be found for inflation? What have been the effects of inflation on welfare and efficiency? To shift the focus, is the economy less efficient than the capitalist economy, as frequently claimed? The evidence bearing on the evaluation of efficiency is of very different types in both economies and easy answers cannot be given. But the research accumulating over the years suggests that the case for inefficiency is by no means as strong as is sometimes thought.

The foregoing and other issues - What is the most meaningful measure of the rate of growth? Is it high and by what standards? What of unemployment? - are analyzed with the help of the very broad range of information that has become available to students of the Soviet economy over the years: Western and Soviet scholarly research, policy documents, Soviet statistics, Soviet newspaper and journal stories and analyses, etc. Gaps remain in this information trove, gaps which preclude final assessment of a number of issues, but for the serious professional economist who has learned that the final word is never in, these need not keep us from a judgment which is more than tentative but less than final, judgments and answers which are couched always within carefully framed questions.

In any book which seeks to evaluate a subject as broad as the workings of Soviet socialism, a writer's debt to other scholars and students in the field must be self-evident. In the present case, besides this general obligation, I would like to express my gratitude for the authors' and publishers' permission to quote in some detail from the statistical research findings of Abram Bergson, Edward Denison (The Brookings Institution), Ivan Koropeckyj, and Simon Kuznets (Yale University Press). I would also like to thank Luis Carresco for his drawings and Muna Salloum for her patient typing of the manuscript. Finally, I would like to acknowledge my indebtedness to Arthur Zapolsky Arnold, my first tutor in the arcane field of Sovietology and in a wide range of other areas of economics and statistics. Professor Arnold's study of the Soviet money and banking sector was one of the earliest scholarly treatises in the field, and his breadth of learning and scholarship provided a keen inspiration and stimulus to embark on a scholarly career.

A.A.
Toronto, Ontario, 1979

1 Introduction

The title of this book - Economic Evaluation of Soviet Socialism - was carefully chosen. The book does not concentrate on the Soviet economy in general, an economy whose structure and performance are conditioned by, among other factors, the climate, geography, and history of that nation and its predecessors. Nor do we study socialism in general, a subject whose definition is surrounded by ambiguity and controversy. Rather, we study the Soviet brand of socialism, which may differ from that in other countries where it may be called socialism or communism, and may also differ from earlier brands of communism and socialism.

DISTINGUISHING CHARACTERISTICS OF SOVIET SOCIALISM

To gain an appreciation of our topic, and a feeling for the extent to which generalized conclusions may be made, brief remarks on some ambiguities in the definition of socialism will be of value. What is "socialism"? And in what ways is Soviet socialism a distinct form of organization.

Two people rarely mean the same thing when they refer to communism or socialism. In a news story in the mid-1970s a major international newspaper reported that the Allende government in Chile was a socialist and not a communist government. The reactions of one used to thinking of these terms within the context of the Soviet Union would be: "That is hardly a comfort; the USSR is also a socialist rather than a communist government. But the USSR is a major political-military threat." On the other hand, the probable reaction of one accustomed to thinking in a Western context would be: "Well, Allende could not have been so bad in that case. After all, England had a socialist government too." On the other hand, the reported attempts of the United States CIA to destabilize the socialist government in British

1

Columbia in the mid-1970s suggest that some Western officials, at least, tend to confuse even mildly socialist forms of organization, within what is essentially a capitalist context, with socialism Soviet style, i.e., a potential enemy.

Thus, we have a situation in which socialism is all right, except if it is not: in which the Soviet Union, to some observers, is not a communist nation while it is a socialist nation; whereas to others, it is a communist nation, while it is not a socialist nation. In a sense, both are right: in the Soviet usage, the USSR is in a transitory state between capitalism and communism - more precisely, full communism - and the transitory state is termed "socialist." The word is incorporated in the country's name, the Union of Soviet Socialist Republics. But when the contrast is to the Western capitalist world rather than to the ultimate state of perfect communist organization, it is termed a communist country. But if Soviet socialism is to be contrasted with the Western world, in which case we speak of communism vs. capitalism, we must first ask in what way besides geographical location it is different. What are the distinctive features of socialism or communism and capitalism?

It is possible to distinguish socialism from capitalism according to various criteria. Probably the one most relied on is the ownership of the means of production. In a socialist society the means of production are owned by the state, whereas in a capitalist society they are owned by private individuals. Unfortunately, a great many exceptions undermine the identification of public ownership with socialism. First of all, in socialist states such as the USSR or other Eastern European economies, many small tradesmen own their means of production, and collective farmers cooperatively, but privately, own their equipment. But, more vexatious is the large number of exceptions among the many Western capitalist nations in which the state owns a vast share of the means of production. In many nations, such as France, Brazil, or Mexico, commonly held to be typical examples of capitalism, the state sector accounts for a larger and larger share of the means of production as time passes. Sometimes the basic means of production are owned directly by the state; sometimes they take the form of public companies with independent balance sheets. Even in the United States, a large share of the means of production is state-owned - highways and public energy are two ready examples.

Attempts at classification are further complicated by anomalies such as Yugoslavia which claims that it alone is a socialist nation since only there do the workers truly own the means of production directly, rather than indirectly through the apparatus of the state as in the Soviet Union. This distinction is in line with the ideas of many nineteenth century socialist thinkers. According to the prevailing Yugoslav view, the Soviet Union is not a socialist state at all, but simply a variation of capitalism, with the state being cast in the role of capitalist owner of the means of production. On this definition the traditional geographic classification of economic systems, in which Eastern Europe, the Soviet Union, and China constitute one type of economic system while the Western world represents another, could not be accepted. (Indeed, Cuba had already upset that criterion, as did

Chile of the early 70s, although subsequent events have restored part of the earlier simplicity).

What other characteristics can be invoked as distinguishing hallmarks of socialism and capitalism? Several features of the capitalist mode of production have been observed historically, but most of these are characteristics of industrialization rather than peculiar features of capitalism. We will look at the most important of these.

1. Increasing specialization of labor and the roundaboutness of production with capitalism were associated by Marx but these are characteristics of any industrial state. Since capitalist states industrialized before socialist states, these features of production have typified the capitalist mode of production longer than the socialist mode.

2. The extensive use of money has been a feature of capitalist development, but, again, this is really a characteristic of commercial states and of industrialization. The fact that the monetized sector is more pervasive in capitalist economies than in socialist economies really reflects the greater industrialization of capitalist economies. For example, a large part of the agricultural sector in socialist nations is marked by payment in kind; but this is also true of lesser developed nations generally, whether capitalist or socialist.

3. Since many socialist economies are "command economies" with a dictatorial structure, it is not unreasonable to think of dictatorship as a distinguishing characteristic of socialist economies. However, there have been enough examples of capitalism with dictatorship - Mussolini's Italy, Hitler's Germany, and many less developed dictatorial capitalist countries today - to undermine this assumption.

4. The presence or absence of economic planning has sometimes been thought to provide a contrast between capitalist and socialist economies. But France and Brazil, capitalist economies with a large amount of central planning, and Yugoslavia, a socialist nation with practically no central planning, provide significant counter-examples.

Evidently, then, we cannot hope to define socialism unambiguously in terms of institutions and rules of behavior. We can, however, analyze the socialism of the Union of Soviet Socialist Republics, itself a topic of great importance, from six major viewpoints (see Section 2 below). What are the main features of this brand of socialism? Five important characteristics have distinguished Soviet socialism histori- cally: (i) revolution and complete overthrow of the pre-existing order to institute a new society; (ii) public, i.e., state ownership of the means of production; (iii) a continuing non-democratic, authoritarian regime; (iv) rapid industrialization based on a very high rate of investment; and (v) a nominal commitment to equity and social justice, subject to the constraints imposed by the nation's other goals. These characteristics distinguish the Soviet economy from socialist economies such as Yugoslavia, as well as from non-socialist regimes such as Brazil. Other characteristics of Soviet development and organizational structure, such as collectivization of agriculture and the central planning mechanism which do distinguish it from some socialist economies, were not included in the list above since they are thought subordinate or adventitious rather than inherent characteristics of the Soviet state. Thus, many leading observers of Soviet economic development have been persuaded that collectivization was necessary to permit exploitation of agriculture to support industrialization. On the other hand, it is conceivable that, while such a characteristic may have been necessary historically within the context of the more closed Soviet economy, it may now be quite inessential in smaller economies that can rely more on foreign trade, with the socialist bloc as well as the capitalist world. Since one of the many sources of interest in the study of Soviet socialism is as a model for economic development, it is important to keep those characteristics of the economy that might not have to be mimicked by countries developing today separate from those features which are basic or essential. Similarly, the large central planning apparatus is probably not an essential feature of Soviet socialism, although it has played an extremely important role in the Soviet economy. But other modes of operation and other ways of supervising enterprises are being increasingly developed so that, again, it might be unnecessary for countries now developing to adopt this aspect of Soviet organization.

SOURCES OF INTEREST IN THE STUDY OF SOVIET SOCIALISM

Economic analysis of Soviet socialism is informed by several distinct points of view. It is essential that these be kept distinct, that we guard against applying a conclusion which is arrived at when performance is assessed from one point of view to the evaluation of Soviet socialism from a different viewpoint which requires different criteria. The following six major sources of interest in the evaluation of Soviet socialism should be distinguished.

Size and Military/Political Strength

The Soviet economy is generally recognized as the second most powerful economy in the world today. This great strength has been and is being used throughout the world to back up foreign policies which may or may not themselves have an economic objective. One specific issue, of course, is the military potential that economic strength provides. For this issue one must analyze the way in which military needs are influenced and directly constrained by economic considerations and variables. Thus, there is a relationship between economics and foreign policy; but equally clearly, approval or disapproval of economic characteristics of the economy, such as income distribution or the rate of growth, may have little to tell us about the country's ability to pursue any particular policy.

Foreign Trade

The large size also directly affects foreign trade. While for most of its history the Soviet Union has not engaged heavily in foreign trade, especially with the West, the prospects for growth of this activity are imposing, and this trade has grown sharply since the early 70s. United States-Soviet trade turnover has been growing by as much as 100% per year, excluding trade in grain which, if considered, would multiply this increase.

The First Large Enduring Socialist System

As the first enduring socialist economy, leaving aside such temporary phenomena as the Paris commune or the utopian communities, the performance of this economy has special historical interest.

A Model for Developed Economies

A related issue is the attraction of Soviet socialism for developed economies today. As the communist parties in Western Europe grow increasingly vocal and powerful - those in Portugal, Italy, and France are perhaps the three best examples - countries may soon confront decisions about whether and how to adopt a socialist government and economic structure. While the July 1976 European international conference agreed that every national communist party should be permitted to follow its own leanings and not necessarily be subservient to the communist party of the Soviet Union, clearly any incoming socialist government in an industrialized country will wish to adapt, if not adopt, the Soviet experience; moreover, this experience may even weigh heavily in the democratic decision making process in determining whether the local communist party can form a government.

A Model of Economic Development

Guided by the forced imposition of the dictates of a small ruling class which, at the start at least if not faithfully and continually over the years, was guided by a genuine concern for social progress, justice, and economic industrialization, Soviet socialism holds out great promise to the developing world as an alternative to traditional reliance on market forces. As less developed countries continue to make relatively little progress through reliance on traditional capitalist forces, especially in improving income distribution even when they do achieve respectable growth records, the Soviet example has gained and will continue to gain many adherents.

Consistency with Marx's Views

While this viewpoint may be of interest principally to academics and, among academics, principally to those concerned with the interpretation and transmission of Marx's thought, it is also relevant for policy makers to know whether the pervasive subscription to Marxist belief within the Soviet Union may impose constraints on Soviet political and economic policies - income distribution, price formation, foreign relations, foreign trade. It is important, therefore, to determine the consistency of Soviet development with the Marxian model in the past in order to evaluate the ideological constraints on its evolution in the future and, from this, to try to determine the extent of such constraints on the workability of socialism in general.

As we noted, we must keep these sources of interest in the Soviet economy distinct. For example, it would be one thing to conclude that people in a Western, industrialized economy might not, after all, be any better off under a socialist government; however, people in a less developed country might find the Soviet road, or some part of it, the only way to achieve anything like social justice and economic progress for the masses.

ISSUES TO BE STUDIED

The aspects of Soviet performance which will concern us in this brief monograph are dictated by the six sources of interest in the study of Soviet socialist performance just presented, and divide neatly into three kinds of issues: 1) organizational-structural aspects; 2) growth; and 3) efficiency.

Organizational-structural aspects of the economy relate to the ability of the economy to cope with the host of problems that confront any modern economy and the ability to achieve the goals which are usually thought to be desirable. For example, does the economy demonstrate any special capacities to reduce inflation? If it does not, does it matter? May the economy have been able somehow to obviate the traditional undesirable consequences of inflation? May other problems have been introduced? Is there an unemployment problem? Has the business cycle been overcome? What of income distribution - what are the goals and how well are these achieved? What of other mechanical aspects of the economy, such as its executive ability, ability to get important things done? These questions are the subject of Chapter 2.

Chapter 3 analyzes the growth of the economy and of important macroeconomic aggregates, such as national income, industrial production, consumption, and output per man. Over the years a wide variety of measurements and methodologies have been employed, and we indicate which are most relevant and meaningful for the major viewpoints of interest.

Chapters 4 to 7 are devoted to the analysis of economic efficiency. Whatever the Soviet economy may have achieved may be too high or too low, a target for some other economy because of different resources, histories, climates, and so on. One extremely important aspect of Soviet performance is the degree to which it has been efficient in its operations and growth. As every economist is aware, it is easy to talk about efficiency; it is easy to depict it in a simple two-dimensional diagram. But it is much more elusive variable to study than, say, growth of national income, whose study is itself a momentous challenge. It is equally clear that evaluations must be made for an economy contemplating organizational alternatives, since it is efficiency - the ability to achieve in relation to what may potentially be achieved - rather than the achievement itself that must enter such decisions. Accordingly, in these chapters we analyze the economy's efficiency through analysis of four extremely critical sectors and aspects of performance: transportation and location, agriculture, industry, and the price mechanism.

In Chapter 4 our concern is spatial efficiency. The complex and intertwined issues of economic location and transportation are separated as carefully as possible to try to answer whether either or both has been the source of waste in the economy and where responsibility for the record lies. Chapter 5 analyzes agriculture to separate the systemic features of the traditionally low agricultural output levels of the Soviet economy from features that may simply be due to climate, or the long and sharp politically given preference for development of industry. Chapter 6 surveys the evidence bearing on efficiency in industry. The evidence is of very different types and quality, ranging from behavioral assumptions and expectations to formal definition, and measurement of productivity change to analysis of individual industries. In all our judgments and conclusions, comparisons with the record and with beliefs and expectations concerning Western capitalist economies are held constantly before us.

One of the most frequently cited causes of inefficiency in the Soviet economy is the price system, heavily influenced by Marxian precepts which are generally believed to preclude the kind of economic efficiency that a free market, with its notions of supply and demand, is believed to promote. Chapter 7 contains an analysis of this mechanism and its influence, and contrasts it with the operation of the price mechanism under capitalism which itself is seen to be far from satisfactory.

Finally, Chapter 8 summarizes the evidence of the earlier chapters from the major viewpoints of interest to this book.

2 Organizational and Structural Characteristics

The Soviet Union has been both criticized and applauded for the institutions it has developed to cope with various micro- and macro-economic aspects of the economy and the results it has achieved. In this chapter we will evaluate the evidence concerning control of business cycles, employment, inflation, income distribution, and executive ability, i.e., the ability to implement decisions.

CONTROL OF CYCLES

In his analysis of capitalism Marx laid great emphasis on the business cycle as a source of weakness in the economy, and built his model of the downfall of capitalism upon successively more severe swings. In the years since World War II, however, the severity of business cycles in the capitalist world has diminished rather than increased, so much so that by the early 1970s it was not at all uncommon to find thoughtful newspaper articles suggesting that the business cycle was a thing of the past. This applies to cycles in absolute terms, at any rate, although decreases in macroeconomic activity in per capita terms might still be observed. This view was also evidenced in articles in scholarly journals that reformulated the Marxian analysis in terms of per capita rather than absolute levels of activity. The subsequent experience of 1975-6, however, when many leading Western industrialized nations did experience a recession in absolute terms, does suggest that the optimism was premature.

What of the Soviet economy? Has it managed to eliminate economic swings? The answer appears to be in the affirmative. Although one Western analyst in an interesting study of fluctuations in the Soviet economy has shown that there has been variation in the rate of year-to-year growth in one major sector of the Soviet economy, industry, it would be very difficult to argue that the absolute level of industrial

8

activity itself has been subject to ups and downs. In his analysis, Raymond Hutchings (1969) shows that during the prewar period 1920-1940 the year-to-year change in the annual rate of growth of output (but not the level of output itself) ranged from .7% to 66.4%. That is, there was a pattern of cyclical variation in the rate of change of output rather than in the level of output itself.

Since World War II, there has again been variation in the year-to-year differences in annual industrial activity, which decreased from +25% in 1948 to 12% in 1954, and to 8% in 1966. Thus, the annual rate of growth in industrial output has become very stable, and over the years there has almost never been an absolute decrease in industrial output, the variation being limited to the rate of growth of output, rather than its level. Much of the variation in the prewar period can probably be attributed to the tremendous pressures being imposed on the economy and the novelty of the situation. This is especially so during the NEP when the growth rate varied from 14% to 67% and when industrial growth (recovery) was the greatest. Subsequently, during the first three plans, these factors combined with the purges probably suffice to explain the variation in annual growth, although it was much lower by that time. Since then, as noted, fluctuations even in the rate of growth appear to have been eliminated.

It is important to stress that this analysis refers only to industrial output. Taking account of agriculture as well would probably magnify the variation in annual growth rates before World War II because of the depredations and reactions caused by collectivization, as documented by Naum Jasny, Alec Nove, and many others. During the postwar period, taking agriculture into account would probably increase the variation in annual growth somewhat, but certainly not to the same extent as in the prewar period. Then, agricultural fluctuations, primarily attributable to collectivization and weather, were much less sharp than those in industry and resulted in a relatively stable performance for the whole economy. Thus, from official figures for agriculture reported in Narkhoz (1922-72), the sharpest year-to-year change in total agricultural production was 28% in 1947, and the largest relative difference in the annual changes was -22% in 1936. Total agricultural growth was remarkably stable through the early 1930s in spite of collectivization, although the livestock-crop composition changed sharply. But for the entire 50-year period, the picture that emerges shows a fair degree of stability in the year-to-year rate of growth.. All figures are unadjusted Soviet data, such as were the basis for Hutchings' analysis, and will be evaluated in Chapter 3 we evaluate these Soviet data together with independent Western estimates to answer questions about growth rather than short-term changes.

The main interest in studying fluctuations in the West arises out of concern with the effects on the income of the workers. In the West, much of the impact of cycles on employment and income has been vitiated by the introduction of unemployment insurance and other programs. To be sure, we may still be interested in the morale of workers, which does begin to degenerate after months of inactivity even though income continues, and it is these more fundamental aspects -

unemployment and psychological well-being - that we are interested in rather than the fluctuations themselves. Unemployment can be studied directly, however, so that we need not rely on indirect measures and variables such as short-term industrial swings. As will be seen, unemployment is a very minor problem in the Soviet economy, so that the income effects related to unemployment may be neglected. On the other hand, the effects of inflation on income or other characteristics of the economy will have to be considered at the appropriate place.

UNEMPLOYMENT

In any modern industrial or industrializing economy, three kinds of unemployment must be dealt with: 1) unemployment due to cyclical fluctuations and 2) persistent large pockets of secular unemployment due to the inability of large population groups to develop or upgrade skills and integrate into the industrializing sector, as is seen among workers in the town-to-country migration in Third World countries, and 3) technological unemployment resulting from changes in production processes, such as the shift from coal to petroleum as a fuel base and the corresponding reduction in coal mining. What is the picture with regard to these kinds of unemployment in the Soviet economy?

We consider first cyclical unemployment, the area which has attracted most attention because of Marx's analysis and because of Soviet criticism of unemployment in Western economies while at the same time maintaining that in the Soviet economy there is no unemployment, a claim usually accepted with a great deal of skepticism by Western writers. In fact, in the absence of sharply defined cyclical fluctuations, which we saw above to be the situation in the postwar period, it would seem reasonable to accept the Soviet assertion that no cyclical unemployment exists. For the 1930s, while industry was increasing every year at highly variable rates, unemployment may have been more severe. However, labor turnover in industry was very high at that time, reaching 1.5 in 1932 when workers held their jobs on the average of 8 months (Holzman, 1960) because of the competitive bidding for workers and in spite of various administrative obstacles which the state was imposing on their movement. The labor force (non-farm population) in this 1928-1940 period grew 175%. (Jasny, 1961, p. 447), and there is no evidence that these workers were oversupplying industry even in years in which the rate of industrial growth fell sharply.

In the pre-plan era - most of the 1920s - there was high unemployment, estimated by Maurice Dobb at two million, which may have amounted to 15% of the urban labor force. It was due primarily to the rapid inflow of workers from the countryside, where according to S.G. Strumilin, an eminent Soviet economist (Dobb, 1948, p. 189), they comprised a pool of 8 or 9 million unemployed workers. But this was a transitory characteristic of the economy and not a lasting or even a recurring feature.

The picture regarding cyclical unemployment, then, appears to be rather good, i.e., there is very little. No estimates have ever been produced by Soviet writers, but all considerations suggest that that is unimportant.

To the extent that frictional unemployment (short-term unemployment due to residential relocations or connected with job search for upgrading) does exist, it is extremely low, almost certainly less than 1%. (The target rate of 3-4% unemployment in many advanced Western capitalist nations corresponds to frictional unemployment.) To the extent that this low-level unemployment does exist, however, we must note that there is as yet no provision in the system for unemployment compensation. On the other hand, since such frictional unemployment may be assumed to be very short lived, the loss in income is not consequential. It is also noteworthy that while unemployment compensation is not paid, there are provisions for disability benefits, and in recent years these have grown substantially, doubling between 1965 and 1972 (Narkhoz 1972, p. 728). These are for temporary disabilities, with benefits of 100% pay for work-incurred injuries, and 50-100% for non-work-incurred disabilities, the amount of benefits depending on years of service (Brown, 1966, p. 363).

Concerning secular unemployment, the Soviet picture again appears good. While to be sure there may be some disguised unemployment or less than fully utilized employment in the agricultural sector, either in its present situation or as it would operate under greater education and worker technical skills (see Chapter 5), there is nothing like the huge numbers of unoccupied workers migrating to and massing in the cities, such as is found in many if not most developing economies today. Thus, while workers may be used below their full potential in agriculture or even, possibly, in industry, they are at least employed; thus the social and economic problems common to most other developing countries have been avoided.

Finally, in regard to technological unemployment, this does arise from time to time or in isolated regions in the Soviet economy, as it does in all other countries. The labor unions represent a force to ameliorate such occurrences, however, by relocating workers while helping them find new employment. According to Emily Brown: "...when technical or organizational changes reduce the need for labor, a major protection against unemployment lies in the reluctance to displace workers without assuring them other jobs or needed training" (Brown, p. 315). To some extent, then, forced retention - either legal or moral stress, on worker retention - is one means to cope with potential unemployment, but this would necessarily affect labor productivity.

While such constraints against discharging workers may have an adverse effect on productivity, they are probably less severe than certain counterpart measures in the West. For example, in the West resistence to technological change to preserve jobs in construction is frequently built into zoning codes, which respond with only very great lags to innovations in building materials, technology, and assembly operations. Ironically, of course, many of the innovations are themselves brought about by restrictive work practices. Obviously, it is also extremely difficult to measure the effects here, as it would be in the case of Soviet productivity. However, as we will see in the analysis of macroeconomic productivity aggregates in Chapter 3, Soviet productivity has performed well in the economy as a whole in comparison with the United States.

To sum up, the employment picture in the Soviet economy is good. There is virtually no cyclical unemployment, no secular unemployment, and only a little technological unemployment. Disability-related unemployment is compensated. The little non-compensated unemployment that does exist is probably of short duration. The total impact of unemployment on social stability is undoubtedly slight since there is so little unemployment, which contrasts sharply with persistent secular unemployment, especially when it is reinforced by cyclical unemployment in the West. Effects on productivity from certain legal and moral obstacles to increased unemployment are unquantifiable, as they are in the West where, however, they may well be of greater consequence.

INFLATION

In the past two decades inflation has ceased to be viewed as an unmitigated evil in the West. In economic development policy, at least, a school of thought has developed which holds that inflation is not only an inevitable consequence of the sharp structural transformation that development implies, but also can provide a critical stimulus to economic development. This view, of the so-called "structuralist" school, argues that inflation is especially important to re-orient the interest of wealth holders from agriculture to industry. The mechanism is essentially as follows: under the influence of industrialization policies, the demand for industrial workers rises, wages increase, and profits and relative prices of capital goods also rise. But besides the shift in relative prices, the average absolute price level starts to rise, the monetary authority expands the money supply, and industrial prices continue rising. Meanwhile, agriculturists start to shift their activity into industry, reinforcing the industrialization process. Numerous variations on this essential theme have been developed. (See, for example, the relevant chapters of Baer and Kerstenetzky, 1964). It is easy to find empirical examples which bolster the structuralist argument, most notably Brazil during the 1950s, and again since the late 60s. Further support of the thesis is found in the existence of many countries with low inflation and low growth - many middle eastern and African nations. On the other hand, numerous counterexamples can also be adduced to impugn the structuralist argument: in Latin America, Chile and Argentina are examples of low-growth, high-inflation economies, while Mexico is an example of high growth with low inflation, as was Iraq in the 1960s, a half-world away.

Thus, the final evidence concerning the structuralist position is still inconclusive, although it does not appear to be terribly persuasive; the consequences of inflation in other circumstances do appear to have stronger impact on the real economy, however. In most capitalist economies, inflation has significant effects on the distribution of real income, traditionally harming those on fixed income, such as pensioners. Since this can be, and in recent years has been to some extent, mitigated by tying pensions to a cost of living index - indexation - these undesirable effects may be offset. Incidentally, on the other hand, if indexation is carried too far, the informational content of changes in relative prices may also be vitiated. (For a brief discussion of this effect of indexation see Abouchar, 1975). The tax structure can also be used to offset the shift in revenue to the public sector which would otherwise follow from inflation, although with very rapid inflation - 15% a year or more - owing to the progressive income tax rates of most advanced industrialized nations, such a shift in revenue can probably not be altogether counterbalanced. While many politicians would view such failure to offset the shift in revenue to the public sector as an advantage, an analyst with a welfare economics orientation must ask whether such a result would indeed lead the economy to a higher welfare level. Which of these or other effects of inflation have been or are likely to be observed in the Soviet case? And how serious have they been?

Although it is a planned economy, and at times has devoted great attention to financial and monetary magnitudes, the Soviet economy has always suffered inflation, though at times muted. Inflation was especially strong during the early years of civil war, war communism, and the early NEP, in which the price level rose between 1913 and 1924 by nearly 62 billionfold (Arnold, 1937, p. 187). During the 1930s, fastidious supervision was exercised over monetary policy, but price levels still rose sharply: industrial goods prices rose 100% between 1928 and 1939, industrial wages over 400%, and consumers goods prices by 700% and 1700% in state-cooperative stores and collective farm market outlets, respectively (Holzman, 1960, p. 167). Following World War II inflation continued through 1956, the foregoing price categories rising by approximately 150%, 150%, 100%, and 50% by 1956, respectively (the collective farm market price index reached levels over 300 times higher than the 1928 prices during World War II). (1) During the 1960s and early 1970s wholesale prices (including turnover tax, and excise tax), have been remarkably stable, (Narkhoz, 1972, p. 197). This applies both to the overall wholesale price index in industry and the wholesale prices for light industry, food industry, and heavy industry.

Indexes of prices net of turnover tax have also been extremely stable since the late 1950s, although there is some evidence of rising consumer prices. Increases in nominal wages were sufficient to offset these increases, however. According to official statistics, average real wages (of workers and employees, i.e., essentially neglecting collective farmers who are considered by the state to be working on their own account rather than as hired labor), rose by 72% between 1960 and 1972 (Narkhoz, 1972, p. 535). The real earnings of collective farmers undoubtedly paralleled these overall averages. But this is really not the point since the serious problem of inflation that we are considering here is the reduction of real income of those on fixed nominal income, so little information is shed on this issue by considering changes in the real income of income earners. Yet there is very little information available on pension rates and other fixed nominal income levels to permit us to say as much about this issue as we would like. On the other hand, given certain institutions in Soviet society, including the heavy subsidies of food products and housing, this aspect of inflation has probably been avoided to date, or at least, has been much less serious than the deteriorating position of fixed income groups in North America during the late 1960s and 1970s.

While real wages did rise in the postwar period, they had fallen sharply during the prewar period, with price increases far outstripping wage increases. According to Janet Chapman's calculations (1963, p. 145), real wages fell by 20-55% between 1928 and 1940, depending upon the choice of cost-of-living index and on whether or not taxes and bond subscriptions are included. However, it would be more correct to ascribe this deterioration in living standards to the decision to industrialize rather than simply to price inflation: in effect it was determined that only a decreasing share of total output could be devoted to consumption; the wage to workers, which essentially expresses the ratio of available consumer goods and services to the amount of work time expended, would obviously have to fall.

There was one important and quite unexpected consequence of Soviet inflation, however. This had to do with the peculiar procedures which came to be employed for assigning prices to new products. For purposes of measuring national output, it was decided at an early stage of industrialization to adopt so-called constant prices of the fiscal year 1926/27 (before 1931, the Soviet fiscal year ended in October; in 1931 it was shifted to a calendar year). This was reasonable in principle since, by the time the first five-year plan began, prices for the year prior to the year of adoption of the plan would have been generally available. Besides being used in the measurement of aggregate national output, however, the prices came to be used to control the performance of individual enterprises.

In a setting of such rapid industrialization, difficulties always arise in the assignment of prices for new products which were not produced during the year on which the constant prices are based. In principle, the resolution of the problem should offer no serious difficulty: it would simply be a matter of determining the prices for the inputs that existed in 1926-27, calculating the total inputs of the respective materials necessary for the new product, and summing to derive the 1926/27 equivalent price, i.e., the price that would have prevailed if the product had been produced in 1926/27. In practice, one would expect a series of price indexes to develop that could be applied to various input categories, to yield a "constant 26/27 price" even for new products whose technology was not anticipated in 1926/27.

The way the system actually came to be applied departed significantly from this procedure. Industrialization might almost be defined as a process in which there are a vast number of new products, and this would require enormous amounts of bookkeeping and a book-keeping staff. With the industrial labor force growing by approximately

20% annually, labor being attracted primarily from the agricultural sector, and with the tremendous pressures for material production, it was probably inevitable that the staffs of supervisory organs would not be able to keep pace with the needs of the administration, and that niceties such as the use of 1926/27 price indexes would be dispensed with. As we will see in Chapter 3, this neglect introduced tremendous problems for the interpretation of Soviet growth, a problem not recognized by the Soviets themselves, although extensively discussed by Western scholars, e.g., Jasny (1951) and Nove (1957). As Nove shows, this practice encouraged enterprises to produce "new" products, many of which were not new at all, but simply represented minor design changes to justify their treatment as new, thereby generating higher enterprise revenues. Although enterprise performance at the time was not being evaluated strictly in terms of profit and loss, these variables nevertheless did play some role and did provide some inducement to introduce new products unnecessarily.

What was the cost of this phenomenon? We can, of course, only speculate. There may have been many cases in which the economies of learning were sacrificed because of the rapid turnover of new products, and because of the cost imposed further along in the production of wrong products which happened to have higher "constant 26/27 prices." Perhaps, however, the total cost did not loom too large in the overall scheme of things since under such rapid industrialization there would inevitably be so many new products that, even without stretching definitions, most enterprises would find room for updating their product mix. They would then be getting higher 26/27 prices than would be justified by assigning prices to new products based on an input price indexed by the 26/27 index.

We note that Western economies under price controls also display a variant of this phenomenon when firms introduce new designs to justify higher prices than would be permitted by a price control authority. Numerous examples of this, from chocolate bars to violins, were observed in the United States price control experience of the early 1970s.

INCOME DISTRIBUTION

Marx emphasized the exploitation of the proletariat by the capitalist class. The objective of socialism was to redress this inequity and achieve a classless society. From this as well as dicta such as "...to each according to his need," many followers in the Marxist tradition have argued that in a socialist state there would be absolute income equality, although Marx's own pronouncements on the subject were extremely ambiguous. For example, his attempt in the Critique of the Gotha Programme to come to grips with the measurement of labor time, recognizing that workers have different intellectual and physical endowments, different marital status, etc., which require that the right to equal command of the fruits of society "instead of being equal, would have to be unequal" (p. 10) shows nothing if not the complexity of the issue of defining socially necessary labor and equitable distribution. And, following their initial hopes for the institution of communism right after the revolution, the new leaders quickly reconsidered and decided that income incentives had to be employed to propel the economy in the desired direction. The Soviet constitution of 1936 embodied this view with the statement in Article 12: "Work in the USSR is a duty and a matter of honor for every able-bodied citizen, in accordance with the principle: 'He who does not work, neither shall he eat.' The principle applied in the USSR is that of socialism: 'From each according to his ability, to each according to his work.'" The new (1977) constitution retains this view, stating in Article 40 that "The Citizens of the USSR have the right to work, i.e., the right to a guaranteed job with wages corresponding to its performance (quantity and quality) but not less than the minimum level set by the state...."

Explicit recognition of the incentive function of wages has been given many times, and the Soviet wage structure over the years has come to incorporate a number of features which encourage higher output per worker in each skill group, upgrading of skills, attraction of labor to the high priority sectors, and so on. The Soviet wage structure today is an amalgam of rules, procedures, definitions, and coefficients which do conduce to this general objective, i.e., getting workers to make as great a contribution to the economy as possible. The structure has been characterized by Soviet writers on wages in the following way (Kapustin, 1964, p. 286):

> Under socialism where wages are administered in a planned manner, socialist society, proceeding with an eye to the development of the national economy and, hence, the standard of living of all the people, consciously introduces adjustments into the wage level for different industries, to provide a higher wage level for workers with identical skills in the leading industries.

This acknowledgement of wage differentiation by industry, of wages as a tool to attract labor to the needed areas, is repeated in similar words by many Soviet writers on wages, e.g., Kostin (1960, p.25) and, as just noted, has been reaffirmed by the 1977 Constitution. Thus, it is recognized that wages will not be equal. If wages are not equal, the distribution of the fruits of society, which is heavily influenced by the distribution of wages, will also be unequal.

To study the inequality of distribution in Soviet society, we must consider four questions: 1) the distribution of money income before taxes; 2) the distribution of income in kind, such as the consumption of food from private plots on collective or state farms, as well as the other non-agricultural consumption in kind of collective farm workers; (2) 3) the structure of taxes, in order to determine the net income; 4) the extent of non-market consumption, e.g., education, public health, and housing subsidies, and also the consumption "na levo" i.e., the unofficial and somewhat embarrassing side of consumption contingent upon rank, favoritism, and access to foreign channels. The latter appears to be an extremely significant component of upper-class consumption (Katz, 1973; Smith, 1975), although by its very unofficial nature it cannot be introduced explicitly into measures of income inequality, any more than it can be in the West, with which we might wish to make some comparisons.

Regarding a second important issue in the analysis of income distribution - the collective farm sector and income-in-kind generally - there are also difficulties. Although these are not so intractable as the question of unofficial consumption, the questions certainly present problems of conceptual and empirical measurement.

Concerning the income of workers and employees, there have been some ingenious attempts by Westerners to infer or reconstruct the pattern of Soviet income distribution, attempts requiring ingenuity and perseverence because such information is not published by the Soviet statistical authorities themselves. Most notable here is the work of Peter Wiles and Stefan Markowski (1971a, b) in which the wage and salary income distribution in the Soviet Union is compared to that in Poland, Hungary, the United Kingdom, and the United States, and attempts are also made to compare the distribution of total income. According to these studies, the distribution in the Soviet Union is approximately similar to the distribution of wage and salary income in the other nations cited.

There are many ways to measure income inequality. One measure is the interquartile ratio, the ratio of the income above which 25% of the population is located to the income above which 75% is found. Clearly, the higher this ratio, the more unequal the distribution since it means that the income of the top 25% of the people is much higher than that of the lowest 25%. However, neither this ratio nor any other measure is a perfect indicator of income inequality; for example, a country with a high interquartile ratio may have income equality for the middle 50% of the population, while a country with a lower interquartile ratio, may have a very unequal distribution among the middle 50%. Which inequality is more equal? Similar reservations can be expressed about any distribution measure. However, in the case of the interquartile ratio, this particular objection may not be terribly serious, since we would expect that the further apart the extreme 50% of the population, the more spread out would be the middle 50% as well. According to the Wiles-Markowski data (1971b, p. 507) the Soviet Union with an interquartile ratio of 1.8, is not too different from advanced capitalist countries such as the United Kingdom (2.07) or the United States (2.64), and is more or less similar to other socialist economies (Poland 1.8; Hungary 1.75). Wiles and Markowski conclude therefrom that any claims about the elimination of social classes under Soviet socialism, and the eventual attainment of full communism and income equality, are unfounded. However, a number of objections should be raised to such a view, objections based on the other aspects cited above which must be considered in a study of the equity of distribution of society's output. (3)

Our first remark that differences such as that between the United States and the Soviet Union - interquartile ratios of 2.64 and 1.8

respectively - are more significant than Wiles and Markowski appear to recognize. It is, after all, a difference of more than 50%. Thus, while the USSR may be fairly close to the United Kingdom, it is quite different from the United States. But a greater reservation concerns the appropriateness of such comparisons as these in the first place. To be sure, the USSR is today an industrialized giant. But its industrial traditions are rather young: while signs of advanced industry were present in Tsarist Russia, the country under the Tsars was characterized by extreme income inequality, as well as by a generally low level of social progress as compared with countries in the West which had already experienced or were then undergoing a broadly based industrial transformation. Because of this tradition of industry, which is longer than that of most LDCs today, it would certainly be inappropriate to compare the Soviet Union today with a wide sample of Third World nations, which are generally characterized by much wider income gaps than are developed economies; nevertheless, or perhaps because of this difference, the relative equality of the Soviet Union must certainly present a magnet for the poor or troubled intelligentsia in such societies. (4)

The question we would really like to ask is, "Could Tsarist Russia have achieved the kind of income distribution that the Western economies have achieved? Or was it different in such essential respects that, while it could have grown creditably in terms of total output, it could not have achieved even the far-from-equal income distribution that is observed in Western economies?" Is there any way that this question can be answered?

One possible approach is to compare Soviet performance with that of some country that was at the same level of development per capita 60 years ago. One country which comes to mind is Brazil. Although quantitative historical studies are inadequate to answer the question definitively, a number of qualitative aspects of the two countries suggest similar levels of development before World War I, and similar kinds of income and social inequality. Several scholars have studied Brazil's income distribution in the recent past, and concluded that extreme inequalities persist there. According to the study by Albert Fishlow (1972), the Brazilian interquartile ratio in the 1960s was about 13, i.e., over 8 times as high as the Soviet ratio. The Brazilian figure, however, is for wage and salary income, whereas the Soviet measure is for all income. The tax dodgers and unreported "perks," or perks not considered as income, are surely at least as great in Brazil as in the Soviet Union; and "nonwage and salary" income of the high-income groups will be much greater, so that Brazilian inequity is a considerably worse extreme. Add to this the undoubtedly greater income inequity in agriculture, and a picture emerges of income inequity which is far, far greater than that in the Soviet Union.

The final step in the analysis of income inequality is a calculation of after-tax income. Rates in capitalist economies are progressive; they are more so in Western Europe and Canada than in the United States. Meanwhile, the Soviet tax rates are progressive but not as progressive as in Western Europe; the rate on the highest income classes in the

USSR is a smaller percentage of income than in the highest income classes in Western Europe and Canada. But the income of the highest classes has a ceiling much below that of Western Europe, even though, as we noted, the existence of perks and other unreported income does give a ceiling which is higher than that which is officially recognized. The result of all this would be to reduce the income inequality on an after-tax basis in the West European nations, and reduce it much less in the United States. Undoubtedly inequality remains greater in Western Europe than in the Soviet Union, considerably more unequal in the United States and enormously more so in Brazil.

ABILITY TO MAKE DECISIONS OR "EXECUTIVE ABILITY"

The last organizational-structural criterion which we wish to consider is the ability of the economy to make decisions. Two questions are involved: 1) are better decisions made? 2) once a decision is made, is it easier to execute in the Soviet economy than in alternative economic forms? To analyze the first issue, a criterion of "better" is necessary. Economists usually use efficiency as a criterion. Problems in the definition of efficiency and the various approaches to its study are part of the concern in Chapters 3-7. For now we limit ourselves to the easier question concerning the simple ability to execute decisions once they are made.

Within this less restrictive definition, the Soviet "command" economy would seem to have definite advantages over a capitalist system. To be sure, to legislate is not to execute, to prescribe is not to perform, as anyone who is even passingly familiar with problems in marshalling resources in the Soviet economy must be aware. Nevertheless, one cannot but be impressed with the colossal achievements of the Soviet economy in executing policies such as the conquest of space, the realization of supersonic transport, construction of the Bratsk dam, the new Baikal-Amur Magistral (BAM), and so on. Our enthusiasm must always be tempered by the question whether such projects are worthwhile, however, and we must be prepared to question the benefits and costs of such projects. But such problems must be faced in capitalist economies as well, i.e., we cannot assume in a capitalist economy that anything which is done is the correct choice simply because it is done. In the Soviet situation, for example, is the Bratsk dam efficient? The waste inherent in finishing this mighty complex five years before the facilities which could use the power are constructed has been noted by many Western observers. A similar project, the gigantic Ural-Kuznetsk steel combine, is analyzed in Chapter 4. Are the benefits of supersonic transport enough to justify its costs? What of environmental pollution? But we must not leap from raising the question to concluding that they were not justified. Witness the continuing controversy about such matters in the West. The truth is that in the West we are no better equipped to determine the benefits and the costs in terms of pollution than is the Soviet economy.

Essentially, the question we are asking is, even when we are unable to evaluate the economic desirability of a project from an overall social point of view - and frankly, we must recognize that this is frequently the case in the West even when we pretend otherwise - does the Soviet type economy present a better or worse framework for actually getting the job done, and at something like the original cost projection? (We should also note that this itself may not be definitive since the official figure may be understated in order to encourage an affirmative decision to proceed. Would the Soviet Union have been less likely to allow the kind of mismanagement and delays observed in the construction of the 1976 Montreal Olympic facilities due, apparently, to monopsonistic labor unions and administrative venality, leading to cost over-runs of 600-900%, and relying on the use of questionable materials such as the flammable plastic roof in the velodrome? Would a Siberian pipeline be constructed with nearly 4,000 weld imperfections, which could be remedied only at great cost, as was the case in the construction of the Trans-Alaska pipeline? (Like the dam at Bratsk, it has been criticized, and is being increasingly criticized, for its premature construction, for the environmental disruption caused by carrying the oil before constructing the facilities to refine it, so that much of the oil flowing through it in 1978 was exported to Japan.)

These questions have no easy answer. On the other hand the fact that in time of crisis we, ourselves, usually switch to a command type structure, in wartime for example, suggests that many advantages are on the side of the "command principle," which has been an essential ingredient in the Soviet economy.

NOTES

(1) Holzman's work is based on price investigations of a large number of Western scholars and official Soviet sources.

(2) All income components of all collective farm workers must be studied separately since they are not considered "workers and employees" and their income is not included in any statistics which might bear on money income.

(3) Naturally, all such data leave out of account "unofficial" income such as that mentioned in the studies by Smith and Katz already cited, which cannot be quantified in the East or the West.

(4) Of 47 LDCs (countries with less than $750 annual per capita income) contained in a recent study by Montek Ahluwalia (1974), in only one (Bulgaria) do the top 20% in the income pyramid receive less than 40% of total income. In 22 countries, the share accruing to the bottom 20% was less than 12% while the share received by the top 20% was between 52% and 60%. For the Soviet Union the percentage of total income accruing to the top 20% of the population was about 30% (estimated from Rabkina and Rimashev-

skaia, 1972). A wage distribution for workers and hired workers (workers and employees) is given on p. 169. The authors present coefficients showing the relationship between wage income per worker and total income (pp. 214-5), which is fairly stable over income groups. Hence the wage distribution would be close to the distribution of total income.

3 Economic Growth

The growth of the Soviet economy, of individual sectors of the economy, and macroeconomic aggregates has been recorded in official Soviet sources since 1913. The annual statistical year book regularly reports on the growth of national income, consumption, total industrial production, and output of major industries (in natural units, sometimes in money terms, and sometimes in synthetic units such as tractors in horsepower-equivalent units). The analyst may use many of these series directly, although there are frequently problems regarding even some relatively unambiguous series. For example, production of hydraulic cements, a relatively straightforward product as compared with machine tools, say, presents difficulties because it lumps together several types of varying strengths and properties. Here, use of an unstandardized total fails to catch important quality variations (see Abouchar, 1976).

More serious reservations apply to more aggregated measures, such as total industrial production or national income. Because of shortcomings in the Soviet measures, numerous Western investigations have been undertaken in the last 30 years, investigations marked by a great variety in approach and result. Some differences arise because consistent annual data are lacking, while some originate in the inherent conceptual problems which confront the welfare interpretation of macroeconomic magnitudes. This chapter, then, constitutes a guide to and evaluation of the various procedures that have been followed, and is an attempt to select the most meaningful measures to gain an idea of the economy's performance with respect to national economic growth, as well as the performance of such important sectors as consumption or industry.

SHORTCOMINGS IN SOVIET MEASURES OF
MACROECONOMIC AGGREGATES

A major weakness in Soviet macroeconomic statistical reporting is the grossness of data. Many series represent not a total value-added type series but, rather, something like a sales calculation. For example, the total output of industry is reported by summing up the sales of all enterprises to each other, including sales within or between industries. Since there is frequently some misunderstanding about Soviet practice and the different measures employed, it is worth examining them in some detail. The Soviet procedures may be illustrated with the help of Table 3.1, based on a Soviet text on statistical reporting.

To gain an understanding of the meaning and limitations of Soviet macroeconomic statistical measures the reader should try to answer such questions as, "How much of the output of Trust AI is used as input by plants within Branch A?" (1,900). "How much of the input to plant B12 comes from all plants within the same branch as B12?" (600). The reader should follow through the calculations of gross output by the various methods to understand the relationships between the row and column totals.

The official Soviet practice is to use gross output by the plant method, i.e., the grossest of all the measures, to measure two critically important macroeconomic magnitudes: 1) total industrial production, and 2) a measure called the "gross social production" (valovaia obschestvennaia produktsiia). We should emphasize that when Westerners object to the Soviet measure of gross social production, it is not in the sense of its being gross vs. net, as in gross national product vs. net national income, but, rather, because of the plant method by which it is calculated. No such objections would be raised to the gross social production measure if it were calculated by the all-industry method, which would be a very respectable attempt to measure total value-added since it would net out all the interplant flows.

Although the traditional GSP (gross social production) methodology is clearly unacceptable for deriving either a macroeconomic indicator there does exist an alternative macroeconomic measure called, literally, "national income" (natsional'nyi dokhod). Since this measure is calculated by the all-industry method it is an acceptable value-added measure. Indeed, it is this measure rather than GSP which has the longest continuity as a fairly regularly published series. Curiously, however, the movement of the Soviet National Income measure (hereinafter, ND) is surprisingly close to that of GSP, the average annual rates of growth between 1913 and 1975 being 6.7% and 6.8%, respectively, calculated from Narkhoz (1977, p. 77). Thus, while GSP may be artificially inflated many times in relation to ND (the absolute level of neither is published), (1) as long as we are interested in the rate of growth, it would seem that even the GSP measure is as acceptable or unacceptable as ND: if one is good, the other is also, and if one is a bad measure, so is the other. (2)

Thus, this source of criticism of the Soviet national accounts - their

TABLE 3.1. Calculation of Gross Output (Valovaia Produktsiia) by Four Methods

Branch (1)	Trust (2)	Plant (3)	Product (4)	Volume of output of product (5)	Inputs to the production of this product from				Calculation of gross output by method of			
					Own plant (6)	Other plants in trust (7)	Other trusts in branch (8)	Other branches (9)	Plant (10)	Trust (11)	Branch (12)	All Economy (13)
A	I	1	a	1,100	700	300	-	-	2,400	2,700	3,800	7,800
			b	2,000	-	-	-	300				
		2	a	500	300	-	-	-	800			
			c	600	-	200	100	-				
	II	1	c	1,000	500	-	300	-	800	2,100		
			f	300	-	-	100	100				
		2	d	2,000	500	400	500	-	1,800			
			i	400	100	100	-	100				
B	I	1	e	600	-	200	-	100	1,600	2,100	4,900	
			f	1,500	500	400	-	-				
		2	e	1,000	-	300	200	200	1,400			
			g	500	100	-	100	-				
	II	1	e	800	-	200	200	-	1,700	3,300		
			h	1,000	100	-	200	100				
		2	i	3,000	1,000	200	-	-	2,000			
Totals				16,300	3,800	2,300	1,500	900	12,500	10,200	8,700	7,800

Intraplant turnover (5)-(10) = 3,800 = (6)
Intratrust   "   (5)-(11) = 6,100 = (6) + (7)
Intrabranch   "   (5)-(12) = 7,600 = (6) + (7) + (8)
Interbranch   "   (5)-(13) = 8,500 = (6) + (7) + (8) + (9)

Source: A.J. Yezhof, Statistika promyshlennosti, 3rd ed, pp. 94-5.

artificial exaggeration due to double counting - is not so crucial since we can simply use its rate of growth or the rate of growth of ND, which is a net-type measure. We must still make estimates of macro magnitudes, however, because the fact is that the grossness of some of the macroeconomic indexes is only one source of concern, and careful analysis of Soviet performance requires a clear understanding of their other limitations. There are three other major concerns. These are 1) the nature of the 26/27 prices used to weight the output series until the 1950s; 2) the failure of either of the national income type measures to reflect the variety of activities that we include in national income measures in the West, and the resulting incomparability stemming therefrom; and 3) the conceptual problems and ambiguity in interpreting the growth record of any macroeconomic magnitude with constant price weights when relative prices undergo drastic change. Beside the major problems, other reservations concerning the meaningfulness of Soviet prices have been expressed by Western writers, since the rationale underlying them does not have the same theoretical foundation as do prices in a free market for measurement of the well-being or welfare of society.

The difficulties arising in the 26/27 prices follow in an obvious way from the discussion of these prices in Chapter 2. Essentially their use means that the price weights used to measure output were not constant but, rather, inflated. Thus, looking at any series expressed in "constant 26/27 prices" would be like measuring GNP in the West in current dollars: such practice would surely not have provoked serious consternation before 1970, when the inflation rate was probably not much greater than the statistical error involved in any measurement of income, but used since 1970 it would make a joke of any such calculation, since the rate of inflation has reached 10% or more in North America and exceeded 20% in England. The shortcomings in these 26/27 prices have been discussed sufficiently and need no further elaboration now.

The second source of concern is the coverage of the accounts. In conformity with certain Marxist views of the social value of production, there have for a long time been discrepancies between Soviet coverage and Western coverage. While any international comparison of national accounts is hazardous, it is more so in the case of comparisons involving the Soviet economy than it would be, say, in a comparison between France and the United States, where at least the accounting methodology is essentially agreed upon. In the Soviet economy many services are left out of account. Personal transportation, for example, is excluded as are a number of other service-type, non-material production activities. On the other hand, this would not be as bad as might at first appear since, even for personal transportation, the initial investment in railway passenger cars and fuel costs would get into the national accounts. The only thing omitted would be that which corresponds to the railway enterprise profit which originates in providing the service.

A different aspect of coverage has to do with the coverage of the prices rather than the quantities. Some observers, notably Bergson, have argued that the Soviet prices neglect certain important elements which should be regarded as costs and, conversely, include others which should not be included. Bergson attempts to adjust for these factors, the most notable adjustment being exclusion of the turnover tax, which is an excise tax, and adjustments for capital charges. We will discuss these in the section on national income below.

The third stimulus to independent estimates of national income is the so-called "index number problem," which distorts both comparisons over time and comparisons between nations or regions. The mechanics of the problem are contained in the appendix to this chapter; here we concentrate on its essence which is that, since the prices of goods which are produced in relatively greater amount are relatively lower, a comparison between two situations, say A and B, will almost always show A better, relative to B, when prices of B are used, and the converse. Complicating matters still further is the fact that neither measure is an accurate statement of the "true" change in welfare. (Of course some set of constant prices must be used, lest we get a result in which output becomes larger simply because the currency becomes inflated, which was precisely the trouble with the 26/27 prices.) This problem is the more serious the greater or more radical is the difference between the two situations, as was stated by Alexander Gerschenkron in a well-known passage (1951, p. 47):

> ...one way of describing industrialization is to define it as a process of changing scarcity relationships. At early stages of industrialization, the value of output of certain commodities or groups of commodities constitute a relatively small sphere of the value of aggregate industrial output, while prices of these commodities are relatively high in relation to prices of commodities composing the bulk of industrial output...in the course of the industrialization process it is precisely these commodities whose output expands at a particularly high rate: and this expansion is accompanied by a cheapening of these commodities in terms of the rest of industrial output.

Thus, the two measures will give different results, and neither is strictly true. Two writers, Bergson (1961) and Moorsteen (1960), have derived the unexpected result that, under usual assumptions, the prices of situation B provide a better indicator of the change in the ability to produce the output mix of situation A, and conversely. (See the appendix to this chapter.) In the present chapter we apply this result to evaluate and modify, as necessary, the estimates of the growth of industrial production and of national income which have been developed by Western observers, as well as the official series. The final section of the chapter then builds further on these results and makes some international comparisons of growth. But first we will analyze trends in Soviet consumption.

CONSUMPTION

Soviet consumption per capita remains low by the standards of industrialized Western nations. International comparisons of macro-economic magnitudes always involve serious difficulty, as was indicated in our discussion of the index number problem. Note that we would get ambiguous results even if we knew the social indifference curve (and made the standard assumptions of identical tastes within each economy). Since we do not know these indifference curves, comparisons of consumption levels are still more questionable since we would have to use the actual prices of either country to weight consumption bundles in both countries.

The problem of comparing consumption would apparently be reduced somewhat if we could get closer to physical volumes. The problem of commensurating different goods - bread and bicycles, for example - would still arise. One approach would be to weight the quantities according to work time necessary, on average, to earn the required amount. On this basis, some interesting calculations have been made by Edmund Nash who compared the necessary work time for the consumption of a fixed basket of eight commodities in Moscow and New York in 1959 and 1966. For individual commodities, in 1959 the necessary work time ranged from 50% more (for rye bread) to 2,000% more (for sugar), while clothing work time requirements were 10-15 times greater in Moscow (Nash, 1960, p. 658). The 1966 picture as recorded by Nash continues to show Soviet consumption very low, the work time necessary to feed a basic diet (bread, potatoes, beef, butter, sugar, milk, and eggs) to a family of four having declined only 11% from 1928, and some of the other ratios being less favorable than in 1959 (Nash, 1966, p. 869).

Three reservations to these measures as a gauge of overall relative welfare must be stated at once. First they reflect only a few commodities, but if we included more commodities we would have the index number problem again. We should emphasize that this is not a trivial nicety; prices in part reflect demand, which in part reflects situations which might be completely irrelevant to welfare in the other situation. For example, it is today almost impossible to survive summer in New York City without air conditioning, due to very high residential population densities and its concentration in multi-unit dwellings which exacerbate the effect of high temperatures, while summer in Moscow without air conditioning is still tolerable. The second objection is that, while work time to meet a single family's needs has declined only insubstantially over the period, there are typically more wage earners per family today, raising consumption per family; so welfare evaluations run up against the issue, unanswerable in any society, of trying to separate the psychological and monetary benefits from the physical and psychological costs of working. The third reservation is that even if the welfare of working urban families could be accurately measured, we would still need to know how the number of such families has grown and what has happened to the rest. The total urban population was growing sharply over this period - by 334% between 1913 and 1966 - its share increasing from 18% to 53% of the total (Narkhoz, 1975, p. 7). We can safely say, therefore, that average consumption levels were rising sharply since the urban population and employment in industry were growing so rapidly, as was the consumption of each urban family. To get an idea of total national consumption levels however, we must look at macroeconomic measures. (3)

The major estimates of aggregate consumption are those of Abram Bergson, which rely in part on the investigations of wages, consumer prices, and consumption by Janet Chapman (1963) and others. Bergson's methodology is consistent with the methods which he applies in his other macroeconomic measurements, and it will be convenient to defer remarks and explanations of his methodology in the next section. This is possible and reasonable since, as it turns out, relative prices of the bulk of consumer goods have not changed very much over the years, so that we do not observe vastly different results when early-year or late-year prices are used to weight consumption. The major consumption series, given in Table 3.2, shows a decline in per capita consumption through the 1930s and then an annual increase of 3.1% per capita to 1955, followed by a 4.1% rate of increase from 1958 to 1964. This is certainly a creditable performance but, as noted, consumption levels remain far below those in the West. On the other hand, we must remember that consumption has been forcefully suppressed ever since the inception of planning, with a much larger share of the national output being devoted to investment, the second main aggregate macroeconomic category. This high-pressure investment strategy may have been responsible in part for achieving the consumption growth when compared with most developing and even many developed economies - but this strategy has also created an industrial complex in which consumption may be expected to grow faster at some point in the future. We now turn to the measurement of industrial growth.

INDUSTRIAL GROWTH

The Soviet Union's own measures of industrial output have been expressed most often as a percentage of 1913, the last year before World War I. According to the official index the average annual growth of industry was 10% in the 50 years between 1928 and 1974. But such a rate of growth has never been achieved anywhere in the world, including the Soviet Union.

The major defects in the official Soviet series may be quickly summarized. The first reservation is that the prices used are not constant. The series between 1928 and 1950, when the reported annual growth rate was about 12%, employed the "constant 26/27" prices whose defects have already been discussed. Since 1950, a number of new price bases have been used, without any attempt to dovetail the series by deflating the prices of the new time period to the levels of the prices of the previous period. (For 1939-51, current wholesale prices are used; for 1952-55, prices for the start of 1952 were used; for 1955-67, July 1, 1955 prices; after 1967, July 1, 1967 prices were used.)

TABLE 3.2.   Estimated Soviet Consumption per Capita, 1928-1975

	1950 = 100	Interval	Rate of Growth During Intervals (%)
1928	88.0		
		(1928-37)	(-0.3)
1937	85.3		
		(1937-40)	(-1.0)
1940	82.8		
		(1940-44)	(-10.0)
1944	56.7		
		(1944-50)	9.9
1950	100.0		
		(1950-55)	5.3
1955	129.3		
		(1955-60)	4.2
1960	159.2		
		(1960-65)	2.5
1965	180.5		
		(1965-70)	4.6
1970	226.8		
		(1970-75)	3.2
1975	264.9		

Source: Bergson, 1961, p. 149; Schroeder and Severin, 1976, p. 622.   Per capital consumption estimates for 1928, 1937, and 1944 based on population estimates of Jasny, 1967, p. 447.

Many other objections have been raised to the Soviet index.   One excellent recent survey by Rush Greenslade (1972) cites five principal objections to the index, besides the failure to link the price bases, to wit: i) The plant method is used to calculate the gross value of output. ii) The value of output includes more than finished products.   In particular, inventories of semi-processed work are counted, as is certain industrial repair work.   iii) Pricing of new and custom made products is chaotic.   This is the same problem that characterized the pre-war period.   iv) There is no certainty that product quality does not deteriorate.   v) As an objection to the individual component industry industrial production indexes   - the fact that the industrial classification of enterprises may vary leads to greater apparent growth for some particular industry, merely by including in it firms previously considered part of a different industry. The last problem may or may not affect the overall output measure depending on the supplier relationships. Any overall organizational changes between years will cause the aggregate measure based on the plant method of calculating gross output to reflect simply book-keeping increases or decreases which are unrelated to physical magnitude. On the other hand, since the gross value of output series does in fact move very closely to the ND series, which is a much better attempt at value-added measurement, year-to-year organizational change may not have been very important after all. In this case, the first of the objectives cited by Greenslade would not cloud the interpretation of relative annual changes, although the total level in all years would be inflated as compared to a truer value of output series.

The second of the foregoing objections may also not be too important. We should want inventory accumulation, as well as the intermediate processing on goods which has actually been performed, to be recorded in annual output. Goods in process, of course, should not be valued at the prices of finished products and there is a danger that they are so valued, since it is always somewhat arbitrary to decide precisely what value to impute to goods in process, even on the basis of a cost-of-production approach to pricing policy. However, to the extent that work in process is overvalued, the subsequent incremental contribution to total industrial output which is made when the good is actually finished in the following year will be smaller.

The third problem, that of pricing new products, is of course serious. As we saw, it was sufficiently important in the pre-war period to have been believed to have artificially induced the introduction of new products. This also biases the industrial production index upward. The same thing has been occurring in the postwar period. It is perhaps less dramatic now because of the generally less tempestuous character of the times, but it remains important. It is impossible to determine the net effect of this phenomenon on the performance of the economy. It is interesting to note that between 1928 and 1950, with increases in industrial prices of about 150% and about 400% in wages, the official growth of total output was about 12% annually or 10 times. Between 1950 and 1972, there was an eight-fold increase, but, since the rate of inflation between 1950 and 1972 was much less - less than 100% over the period - a greater rate of real growth between 1950 and 1972 than for earlier years is suggested.

The fourth objection - that product quality is not constant over time - is a trenchant objection to the Soviet index of industrial production, but it also applies to any industrial production index, and is the more serious the greater is the pace of industrialization. We do know that there have been many product quality changes in Soviet industrial production for which the output indexes have not been adjusted - e.g., the stretching of cloth, yielding 10-15% more physical output at the same unit price (Jasny, 1951) as well as the fact that running, rather than square meters are invariably used as the output measure; as another example, consider cement quality variability and the difficulty of taking it into account (Abouchar, 1976). On the other hand, as noted, quality variation is also a serious problem in Western capitalist economies. And it is insoluble, even when intentions are good. For example, a wood frame house today represents a smaller amount of resource input, and hence of production potential, than an all-brick house. The output of the housebuilding industry, if it concentrated on frame houses, would then be larger today than it would if all brick houses were produced, when output is measured in houses, so that the production index of this industry would be higher. On the other hand, if zoning codes had allowed in the base year, frame houses might also have been built at a lower resource input than the number of houses which actually were built, or else we could have had more houses with the same resource input. The increase in measured output then clearly overstates the change in the total production potential of the housebuilding industry. The problem is further complicated by the notion of the utility of the different houses. Does the frame house have the same utility as the brick house? The house may have a shorter life, but that may be unimportant since technological change may make the brick house obsolete in other respects long before its life expectancy is reached. Clearly, the question of adjustment for quality variation is a very difficult one to resolve in the West or East. But Greenslade is quite right that the official Soviet index neglects the question entirely, whereas some Western indexes do attempt to take this into account.

Due to all of the foregoing uncertainties regarding the interpretation of the Soviet measures of industrial production, numerous Western measures have been made since World War II. The main ones are shown in Table 3.3. The periods of observation vary greatly as the interest and objectives of the analyses have varied.

These indexes represent extremely imaginative attempts to measure the growth of total industrial production on the basis of limited evidence. While there are many differences in the indexes, they all have the effect of sharply reducing the Soviet estimated growth rate, as is shown by comparing the estimated average annual rate of growth for the period 1928-1950, as well as by looking at the annual average growth between 1928 and the final year of the study in question. The Seton index, which being very early, was based on the least amount of information, gives the highest growth rate of all the Western estimates over the period for which it is compiled, while the lowest is the Kaplan-Moorsteen index, which uses end-year or late-year price weights and which, in normal circumstances, would have the effect of giving a lower rate of growth in any event (as discussed earlier and in the appendix of this chapter), as indeed is the case. Of all the indexes those which are most nearly similar conceptually are the Jasny, Hodgman, and Nutter indexes, all of which give intermediate growth estimates.

Jasny. This was an attempt to utilize what we might term "real" Soviet "constant 26/27 prices," introducing quality adjustments and correcting for inflation. It is the result of many years of effort by a scholar with encyclopedic knowledge of Soviet sources, organization, and institutions.

Hodgman. This index of total industrial production is an attempt to sum up the industrial production indexes of individual industries, each weighted by its 1934 wage bill. If the production index of some industry

TABLE 3.3. Indexes of Soviet Industrial Production: Major Official and Western Indexes (1950=100)

	Official Soviet Index	Jasny	Hodgman	Seton (1928=100)	Kaplan-Moorsteen	Nutter (all products)	Greenslade
1922	2						
1928	9	21	15	100	27	26	
1932	18	35	27	205	42	36	
1937	39	61	57	463	67	72	
1940	56	74	66	536	71	81	
1945	54	50	41		455	48	
1950	100	100	100		100	100	100
1955	183				158	158	163
1960	300						249
1965	454						342
1970	680						463
1975	966						617
1977	1071 (plan)						

Sources: Narkhoz 1922-72, p. 125; 1974, p. 168; 1977, p. 167
Jasny, 1951;
Hodgman, 1954, p. 89;
Seton, 1958, p. 18;
Kaplan-Moorsteen, 1960, p. 235;
Nutter, 1962, p. 158;
Greenslade, 1976, p. 271.

rose by 500% between 1928 and 1940, and its wages in 1934 accounted for 10% of total wages, its contribution to the index for 1940 would be 9 points.

Seton. One of the earliest attempts to measure Soviet industrial production, Seton's index attempts to infer the behavior of total industrial production from the movement of various physical series, such as ton-kilometers of railroad freight traffic, and the output-input relationships observed for such intermediate activities in other countries.

Kaplan-Moorsteen. This index is based on extensive information studied at the Rand Corporation. New information on machinery production is employed. The index is one of the last compiled and employs 1950 price weights.

Nutter. This index represents the work of a major research project by the National Bureau of Economic Research. Essentially it attempts to use 1928 price weights. It does this by deflating individual production indexes by the relevant price indexes as calculated by Nutter.

Greenslade. This is the most recent index of Soviet industrial growth and is based on 1970 prices.

Which of the foregoing indexes is the most meaningful? As stated earlier, the Soviet index seriously overstates relative industrial production. The variety of results among the others is due to the different methods used and the different price bases. The Greenslade index, which is the most recent, and which covers the longest span in the postwar period, will be most relevant for purposes of evaluating industrial growth possibilities in the near future, especially since relative prices have been reasonably stable over the years he studied. For the assessment of historical performance, however, which may be most crucial for a country contemplating the lure of socialism as a method of economic organization, we must determine which of all the other indexes may be most significant.

First all of them except the Kaplan-Moorsteen index attempt to measure real industrial output in terms of prices of an early year: Jasny's "real" 26/27 prices, Nutter's index which attempts to use constant 1928 prices, or Hodgman's index (and a related Shimkin-Leedy index, not shown in Table 3.3) which, by being based on 1934 wage relationships, implicitly employs prices of that early year. In accordance with the theory of index number relativity and the resulting expectations about the behavior of index number measurements under general conditions discussed earlier, we would expect those indexes expressed in early prices to grow faster than those expressed in late prices. Our expectations are met since the index for the same period expressed in late prices is lower. This is the Kaplan-Moorsteen index.

Thus, the Kaplan-Moorsteen index cannot be compared with the early-year indexes since they are constructed by essentially different principles. The early-year indexes all do show an extremely rapid rate of growth. Indeed, even the late-year indexes although lower, do show a very high growth rate. This is consistent with the analysis of index number relativity. But whichever point of view interests us, the growth rate was enormous and we must conclude that the Soviet economy has performed exceedingly well over the years in question, and leave aside - but only until the next section where we discuss total national income - the question of which is the more appropriate point of view from which to evaluate Soviet production growth.

Before leaving this section, we must caution against interpreting growth in industrial production as growth in the economy as a whole or in consumption. Consumption, which is the macroeconomic variable most immediately related to the current welfare of the population, has grown at a rate only 10-15% as high as the growth rate of total industrial production, both series being measured in terms of early prices. As noted previously, however, the industrial growth index does bear significantly on the prospects for consumption growth in the future. But what rate of growth of consumption can reasonably be expected ultimately? While future growth will be greater than the past growth of consumption, it is unlikely to be as high as the rate of growth of industry itself, which involves the production of producer goods for industry and other sectors. Moreover, total private consumption depends in any event on sectors other than industry - agriculture and the public sector and trade also provide consumption goods and services. These considerations suggest the need to look at more inclusive indicators such as a macroeconomic national income indicator. Besides the hope that this will give a better idea of a steady state equilibrium level of the growth of major economic subsectors, such a measure would be meaningful from the viewpoint of a country assessing the Soviet growth record to decide on the course to follow for economic development. We turn, then, to the measurement of national income growth.

GROWTH OF NATIONAL INCOME

As noted previously, the Soviet Central Statistical Administration publishes data on two major macroeconomic aggregates, which translate literally as "gross social product" and "national income." Their main shortcomings have already been discussed. The major attempt by a Western scholar to reach an independent estimate for the period up to 1955 is the vast body of research undertaken by Abram Bergson (1961) and subsequently updated by Abraham Becker to 1958-1964 (1969); subsequent estimates have been made by other investigators as well, most notably Rush Greenslade (1976). Primary methodological interest here focuses on the pre-1955 period, for which the estimates depend heavily on the price base used for the computations, and on the significance of alternate approaches. Accordingly, the main candidates among which we must choose are contained in Table 3.4, which also contains Greenslade's growth estimates for the 1950-1975 period, as well as the official Soviet estimates.

Bergson's procedures for adjusting prices are described in detail in chapter 8 of his 1961 volume. Bergson attempts to measure national

TABLE 3.4. Soviet National Income: Official Series and Western Estimates

	Official Series (1913 = 1)		Bergson Ruble Factor Cost Series with price of 1937			Greenslade (1970=100)	Synthetic Measure of Growth for Interval (a)	
	National'nyi dokhod	Gross Social Product	1928	1937	"Composite"		Time Interval	Rate of Growth %
1913	1	1						
1922	0.5	0.5						
1928	0.5	n.a.	36.4	61.6	36.4			
1937	n.a.	n.a.	100	100	100		1928-1937	5.5
1940	5.3	5.1	121	121	121		1937-1940	6.6
1945	4.4	4.2					1940-1944 (a)	0
1950	8.8	8.2		150	145	33.8	1945-1950	3.3
1955	15.0 (b)	14.0 (b)		216	209	45.2	1950-1955	6.7
1960	23	21				59.9	1955-1960	5.8
1965	32	29				76.6	1960-1965	5.1
1970	46	41				100.0	1965-1970	5.4
1975	61	56				120.7	1970-1975	3.8
							Average 1928-1975	4.7

(a) For explanation see text.
(b) 1954.

Sources: Narkhoz, 1922-72, p. 47; 1974, p. 51; 1977, p. 77.
          Bergson, 1961, pp. 180, 210;
          Greenslade, 1976, p. 271.

income in terms of prices which he believes are more realistic and more meaningful than the Soviet market prices actually in use. In principle, his prices - the "adjusted factor cost" standard - reflect the true social cost of producing goods. Bergson argues that this standard should reflect the following characteristics:

There should be a net charge for the use of capital goods, i.e., something akin to an interest charge.

There should be a price component corresponding to the differential productivity of land or mineral deposits.

All labor of any given kind should be valued at its marginal product and, of course, homogeneous labor should have the same marginal product or wage within any industry or use. Naturally, this may vary between regions depending on capital endowment, climatic features, and so on.

Perhaps the most important of the implied changes necessary for actual Soviet market prices is an adjustment to allow for major subsidies and indirect taxes, i.e., the turnover taxes which are an excise tax and which do not represent factors of production. Subsidies should also be adjusted for, since they cause the market prices to understate the cost of the factor inputs.

Bergson's principles and procedures have been the source of some controversy although they have been fairly widely accepted by now. Interestingly, the calculations are not very sensitive to some of the particular conventions adopted, the major differences between Bergson's estimates and the Soviet estimates being due to the year for which the price weights are selected and by the mere attempt at holding prices really constant even for a given year, such as 1928. For example, in related calculations Bergson shows that whether or not an explicit charge is introduced as a true capital factor cost component does not make a great deal of difference (1961, p. 140).

Bergson also makes the many adjustments necessary to estimate Soviet national income according to Western national income concepts. The major change necessary here is to allow for the inclusion of services, most of which are omitted from the official concept since, as noted previously, most services are not considered to be part of "material production," to which the Marxist view of Soviet value accords primary and almost exclusive place. Personal services such as passenger transportation are omitted, as well as the services of teachers, doctors, and government employees. The extension of the national income concept to include such activities does not affect the results seriously; there is little difference when Bergson compares his estimates of the growth of a "Western" series with the growth of the Bergson version of the official Soviet concept series, both series reflecting all his other price adjustments. Compared, moreover, with the official series expressed in early prices, the result is to reduce the growth rate by a little more than one-third (p. 180).

There is, however, very great variation in growth for any particular series calculated by the same principles but weighted by prices of different years, much greater variation than there is either between Bergson's "Western" and "Soviet concept" series, or even between Bergson's early-year (1928) weighted series and the official Soviet series, which was also weighted by an early-year (1926/27). Similarly, there is much greater difference between the different series with different price weights than between series calculated with and without interest or capital cost adjustments (Bergson, p. 140). What is the meaning of these results and how should we choose among them?

Clearly, we would expect different results depending upon the year of the price weights used. The 1928-price weighted series gives an indication of the change in the ability of the economy to produce the post-industrialization mix while the series weighted in late-year prices indicates the change in the economy's ability to produce the pre-industrialization mix, according to the Bergson-Moorsteen theory. We note that the three series which use price weights for years after 1936 tend to be similar, suggesting that the radical transformation of the economy took place essentially within the nine years between 1928 and 1937, the little further change in relative prices being evident in the rather muted differences in rates of growth of national product calculated in terms of 1937, 1950 and 1955 prices. But from the viewpoint of an economy considering alternative paths to economic development it would be valuable to express the national income performance of the Soviet Union in a single number. Can we go further with national income measurement or must we inevitably accept two estimates, each answering a different question?

The theory says that the change in capacity to produce the mix of year A is best given by the change in national income when both years are weighted according to the prices of year B, and conversely. However, when years A and B are the beginning and end of a long time it is clear that both of these years will be irrelevant to most of the observations; for any particular year, the scarcity relationships confronting the economy are not those of the terminal years of the experience, but those existing in a given year. We should not expect managers to make technological choices on the basis of relationships of one of the terminal years, but on the basis of those now existing and, if the economy is efficiently organized, we would then expect the prices facing the managers not to be those of either the first year or the end year of the time series. In fact, the manager in a middle year who, while he may have responded efficiently to the scarcity relationships existing at the start of the series, continues to respond to such relationships, i.e., to make technological choices on the basis of cost calculations involving the prices of the starting year of the series, should be discharged for incompetence. An agile manager must adapt and respond to those scarcity relationships which face society today, as measured by today's prices.

An analogy might be made between the desirable behavior of an economy that would grow as fast as possible, subject to the constraint that at the end of the time period the economy continue to be capable of further growth, we might ask a skier to get down a hill in the shortest possible time, subject to the constraint that he can go up again, i.e., that he break no bones. In this case, the critical measure of whether a given skier is fastest on powder or ice, or on southern Ontario corn snow, whether he is expert at negotiating moguls, moving among trees, sliding down faces, or shussing slopes, is not the primary issue. We would not ask how fast he could go down the hill using the particular technique appropriate to any one particular condition that he might meet on the way; rather, we want to know how agile he is in adapting his technique to hazards or conditions which suddenly face him.

The foregoing analogy suggests that we should measure the rate of growth of the economy as the average, over a prolonged period, of the annual growth rates between each pair of successive years, calculated in terms of constant prices of one of those two years. Which year? Following the previous analogy, we want to measure the performance of the economy as it adapts to the changing conditions confronting it. The year-to-year change in output, valued at next year's prices tells us the change in the capacity to produce this year's mix. Since it is this year's mix which we wish to increase, and the ability of the economy to do so is constrained by the scarcity relationships facing it this year, which are in principle measured by relative prices, the path we must follow is clearly indicated - use constant prices of the second year of the two-year pair to form a chain link index. (4)

This approach would require enormous quantities of data, surely unavailable in the correct form even to the Soviet recordkeepers themselves. However, the same approach could be applied to short periods longer than one year. While this has not been done in the past, one of Bergson's series, his "composite" series (1961, pp. 210, 218), can be used to produce such a measure. This series measures the relation between the income in any year and 1937, both valued at prices of the year being compared to 1937. That is, it is a series such as

$$\frac{\Sigma \, Q_{40} \, P_{40}}{\Sigma \, Q_{40} \, P_{37}}, \frac{\Sigma P_{50} \, Q_{50}}{\Sigma P_{50} \, Q_{37}}, \text{ etc.}$$

As such, it tells us the change with respect to the ability to product the 1937 mix, but we really want the change with respect to the mix of each of the end years in the short period being compared, i.e., a series of the form

$$\frac{\Sigma P_{40} \, Q_{40}}{\Sigma P_{40} \, Q_{37}}, \frac{\Sigma P_{50} \, Q_{50}}{\Sigma P_{50} \, Q_{40}}, \text{ etc.}$$

Now, since Bergson's measures in terms of prices either of 1937 or 1950 yield very similar results, prices must have been fairly stable over that period, so that a move to our chain link type index would not make much difference after 1937. Accordingly, to consist with the approach developed here we propose as the single measure of growth between

1928 and 1955 the average of the index for 1928 to 1937 expressed in terms of 1937 prices, and the index for 1937 to 1955 in terms of 1950 prices, the average for each period being weighted in the overall arithmetic average by the number of years in that period of observation. This overall measure is 4.8%, and when further averaged with the rate of growth of the Greenslade series since 1955 (5.0%), yields an average of 4.9% during the period 1928-1975.

It is also of interest to relate the growth in Soviet national income to the growth of population since, obviously, if population is growing at a high rate the implication is a lower increase in welfare than under stationary population. To estimate the per capita growth we first determine the rate of population growth between 1928 and 1975 on the basis of Jasny's 1928 population estimate of 151.3 millions (Jasny, 1961, p. 447) and the mid-year 1975 population estimate of 254.3 millions (Narkhoz 1974, p. 7). This is 1.1%, resulting in a real per capita national income growth rate of 3.8%.

A related source of interest is the estimation of labor productivity and its dynamics over time. Labor productivity is an elusive concept. When working at a macroeconomic aggregative level, we usually think in terms of GNP per man but there are difficulties here cross-sectionally or intertemporally. The problems in comparison of national income per capita, either internationally, or over time, include variation in the work schedule - hours per day, vacation per year, days per week - rather than what we might wish to measure, output per standard input. Other problems involve the recruitment to the labor force of varying qualities of labor, differences in the age structure, and the level of training. For example, should we consider the input of different labor skills as different combinations of capital and labor, the capital representing the investment in the acquisition of skills? Or is it meaningful merely to take GNP and divide it by the number of people in the economy.

Fortunately, most of these problems primarily hamper international comparisons, or comparisons within an economy between widely separated years. The year-to-year change in any of these influences is not likely to be great, so that the labor force can be thought of as reasonably constant over short time periods. Hence, the rate of growth of output per man, measured over short time intervals, is probably more meaningful. Comparisons over a long period of time must come to grips with the problems just mentioned and make adjustments in the observed labor characteristics if we want to get a good comparison between output and a unit of homogenous input.

Bergson has performed calculations of the first type for the Soviet Union and has made comparisons with the United States, based on data of Raymond Goldsmith, with certain further adjustments (pp. 271-6). He makes his major comparisons between the Soviet performance during the period 1928-1955 and two important periods of United States development: the period 1899-1929 which might be considered as the period in United States development which is comparable to this period in Soviet development, and with the period 1928-1950, i.e., essentially the same calendar period as the Soviet case. The latter comparison covers the years of World War II, which affected the two economies very differently. In the United States, these years had the effect of revivifying the economy which had been plodding along, still feeling the depression of the 1930s and carrying it to levels of super-full employment, raising GNP as a consequence. The measurement of GNP is, of course, insensitive to the composition of output, considering a dollar's worth of gunpowder as the equal of a dollar's worth of coffee. With temporarily suppressed personal consumption expenditures accumulating in the hands of consumers and a long backlog of unmet demand, the economy continued at its peak performance in the post-war years. In the Soviet Union, by contrast, the economy was already operating at high pressure before the war, and the war decimated population and wrecked a great deal of the nation's industrial capacity (numerous plants were taken by Germans and many others were despoiled or relocated). Thus, Bergson makes comparisons which include and exclude the effects of the war years.

The comparisons show that Soviet output per man between 1928 and 1955 grew at about 2% annually (2.5% annually omitting the performance of the war years). (5) United States growth was around 1.7% during the 1939-1957 period, applying essentially the same techniques, and 1.6% during the 1899-1929 period which might be regarded as comparable to the 1928-55 period in Soviet development.

Finally, it is of interest to compare the growth of total national income in the Soviet Union with that in other countries.

INTERNATIONAL COMPARISONS OF ECONOMIC GROWTH

On the basis of the estimates just analyzed and the studies of Edward Denison (1967) and Simon Kuznets (1965) we can make several very illuminating comparisons between Soviet growth and that in other industrial nations. Table 3.5 shows the growth rate of GNP and GNP per capita between 1950 and 1962 in ten Western economies, and the Soviet Union. For all these countries we may assume that the relative price structure did not change radically over the period: certainly said changes were nothing like the change in price structure accompanying the process of economic industrialization. The spread of total growth rates is three times (7.2% for Germany versus 2.4% for the United Kingdom) and the spread in annual per capita growth rates is 3.8 times (6.1% for Germany versus 1.6% for the United States). The Soviet growth rates of 4.4% and 3.8% per capita over a much longer period thus constitute a very creditable performance exceeded as they are by only two countries during the 1950-62 period - Germany and Italy. Comparisons for the Western countries over the entire period 1928-1975 would reflect still more favorably on the Soviet growth record, since all the Western growth rates would drop substantially if the depression years were included.

As before, the question would arise of the reasonableness of comparing the Soviet growth record over the period of its industriali-

TABLE 3.5.   Rate of Growth and Per Capita National Income
1950-1962, Major Industrialized Economies

	Average Annual Growth (%)	
	Total	Per Capita
Belgium	3.2	2.6
Canada	7.0	4.3
Denmark	3.5	2.8
France	4.9	3.9
Germany	7.3	6.1
Italy	6.0	5.3
Netherlands	4.7	3.4
Norway	3.5	2.5
United Kingdom	2.3	1.8
United States	3.3	1.6
USSR	5.3	3.9

Sources: European countries from Denison, 1970, pp. 17, 18;
Canada, Statistics Canada, 1963, pp. 6, 10; USSR,
Greenslade, 1976, p. 275; Narkhoz, 1922-72, p. 9.

zation with the performance of already industrialized economies which
may have passed their highest growth periods during industrialization.
However, Kuznets' data on today's industrialized economies, which
reach back to the mid-nineteenth century, do give us a useful basis for
comparison.   Table 3.6 gives the century coefficients calculated by
Kuznets.   These show the growth that would be achieved in a hundred
years if the growth observed in the period of observation were
maintained for a century.   Also shown is that for the USSR for 1928-
1958.   According to this criterion the Soviet performance exceeds the
others in the sample by amounts ranging from 3.6 times (Japan) to 17
times (Australia).   Note that for Kuznets' observations, which are
considerably longer than Denison's, the growth rates are considerably
below those observed during the 12 years of Denison's study.   However,
the periods of Kuznets' study may be too long to be meaningful, since
many non-economic phenomena intrude, particularly the effects of
wars, national realignments, and so on.

TABLE 3.6. Analysis of Long-Term Growth of Per Capita GNP, Major Industrialized Economies

	Based on Long Periods of Observation				Based on Short Period Experience of Table 3.5	
	Period of Observation	No. of Years	Century Coefficient (Times)	Implied Annual Growth (%)	Annual Growth (%)	Century Coefficient (Times)
Australia	1861-5 to 1959-62	98	2.2	0.8	-	-
Canada	1870-4 to 1960-2	89	5.3	1.7	4.3	67.4
Denmark	1870-4 to 1960-2	89	5.9	1.8	2.8	15.8
France	1841-50 to 1960-2	106	5.2	1.7	3.9	45.9
Germany	1871-5 to 1960-2	88	5.2	1.7	6.1	372.9
Italy	1898-1902 to 1960-2	61	5.6	1.7	5.3	174.9
Japan	1879-81 to 1954-61	80	10.4	2.2	-	-
Netherlands	1900-4 to 1960-2	59	3.5	1.3	3.4	28.3
Russia (European)	1860 to 1913	53	3.8	1.3	-	-
USSR	1928 to 1975	47	98.0	4.7	3.9	45.9
Switzerland	1898-9 to 1957-9	64	4.4	1.5	-	-
United Kingdom	1855-9 to 1957-9	101	3.7	1.4	1.8	6.0
United States	1839 to 1960-2	122	4.9	1.6	1.6	4.9

Sources: Kuznets, 1967, pp. 64-5, Tables 3.4 and 3.5; Narkhoz, 1975.

APPENDIX:
GRAPHICAL PRESENTATION OF THE INDEX NUMBER PROBLEM

Figure 3.1 assumes a two-commodity (I and II) economy. The economy is observed in two time periods, A and B, after and before some structural change separated by, say 30 years. Each situation has a given price line showing the relative prices for the two commodities which, when tangent to the corresponding indifference curves, show the optimal point of consumption of goods I and II. These are shown by the points A and B. If the two goods are to be summed to obtain the national income for either year, they must be expressed in commensurable units. This is done by translating one good into the other according to the relative prices P_I and P_{II}. For example, the national income in period A in terms of commodity I is given by Y_{AA}, that of the period B, by Y_{BB}. Each is calculated in terms of its own prices, and the question arises how to compare the two magnitudes to determine the relative income difference.

To measure the difference in welfare between the two situations, we must determine how "far apart" the indifference curves are by some measure that will be proportional to the welfare difference. The approach usually followed is to determine how much income in "after" prices would leave the "before" consumer as well off after the price change as he was before (i.e., on the same indifference curve) and compare this quantity with the income actually generated in the "after" period. One measure of this change is the ratio Y_{AA}/Y_{BA} which represents the true change in welfare and is usually called the "true index number" of the income change between the two periods.

The comparison just made uses "after" prices, but it is just as legitimate to ask about the true change in terms of "before" prices, that is, Y'_{AB}/Y_{BB}. Thus we have two "true index numbers" to measure the change in welfare, and they are both true. In this case they both point in the same direction, although in general they need not. In any event, we do not know the indifference curves - even for a two-product world - and in a real-life multiproduct economy it would be harder still.

What we do do in practice is to weight the observed consumption quantities by the prices. In the case shown in Figure 3.1, we find that the change is positive when we compare the two income levels measured in "after" prices (Y_{AA}/Y_{BA}, which is less than unity, implying a negative change), while it is positive when measured in "before" prices (Y_{AB}/Y_{BB} which is greater than unity, implying positive growth in national income). Thus we may even get differences in sign when we actually perform the measurement by the two methods; at the very least, the differences will be different, possibly very different.

Let us summarize. In practice, we will get different measures of the change in welfare over time. And even if we could determine indifference surfaces correctly in a multicommodity economy, we

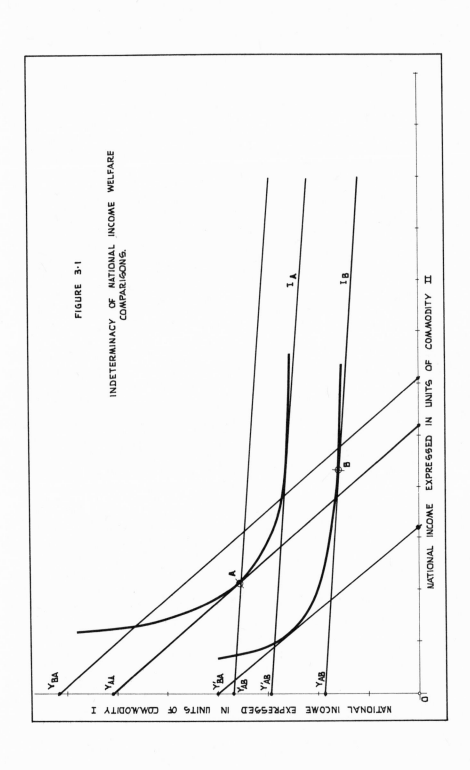

FIGURE 3·1

INDETERMINACY OF NATIONAL INCOME WELFARE
COMPARISONS.

would still have different results depending upon which prices were used. Since we cannot determine these surfaces, possibly a different approach could be tried which would obviate at least this problem. Perhaps the best alternative is the production potential approach of Bergson and Moorsteen, which represents an attempt to get at welfare indirectly, there being a fair presumption that, over the short term at any rate, the amount of goods and services produced is related in a reasonably constant way to the welfare of society. This approach, as elaborated independently by Bergson and Moorsteen, tells us that we must use the other period prices when we wish to measure the capacity to produce this period's mix, i.e., period A prices to measure the change in capacity to produce the period B mix, and period B prices for the change in capacity to produce the period A mix. Following Bergson's presentation, the reasoning is as follows.

Figure 3.2 shows the essentials of the argument for two commodities. Two states are considered, A and B (representing either the same economy at different points or different economies at the same point in time). The concave (to the origin) production possibilities curves of the two states are shown by PF_A and PF_B. Next, price lines, which show the varying quantities of the two goods which have constant value (each weighted by its current price) are shown by D_A and D_B. For example, any point on D_A represents different mixes of food and machinery which have the same money value (the quantities of the two products are multiplied by their respective prices and summed).

The welfare maximizing outputs of the two economies are given by the points of tangency between price lines and the production frontiers, S_A and S_B. How should these be compared? Clearly, the quantities which they correspond to, $S_A = \Sigma P_A Q_A$ and $S_B = \Sigma P_B Q_B$, cannot be compared directly since they involve different prices. We must use constant prices, applying B prices to the A quantities for one comparison and A prices to B quantities for another. To weight the A quantities by B prices is in effect to draw a line through point S parallel to D_B (the broken line, which shows the ratio of the prices existing in B). Any point on this line, labeled here D_{AB}, shows an amount in B prices of the two products which, at the point of actual A production, has a value which is the same as the actual A production expressed in B prices; we are, in effect, converting the actual A production into B units at the price ratio existing in B. Finally, the point at which it cuts the ray from the origin, V_B, shows the value that we would achieve by applying the B period assortment. In other words, the output actually achieved in A, at point S_A, if converted at B prices, into a B mix, is equivalent to the output shown at point T_B. When we compare national income in B prices, using actually observed quantities, then we get a ratio which is equal to T_B/S_B.

Now, as the production frontiers are drawn, following the usual assumptions of concavity, the "true" change in the ability to produce the mix of B is given by T'_B/S_B. As we can see, the ratio given by T''_B/S_B is much closer to this true change than is the ratio T_B/S_B. But T''_B/S_B is precisely what we would get by applying the prices of state A to both

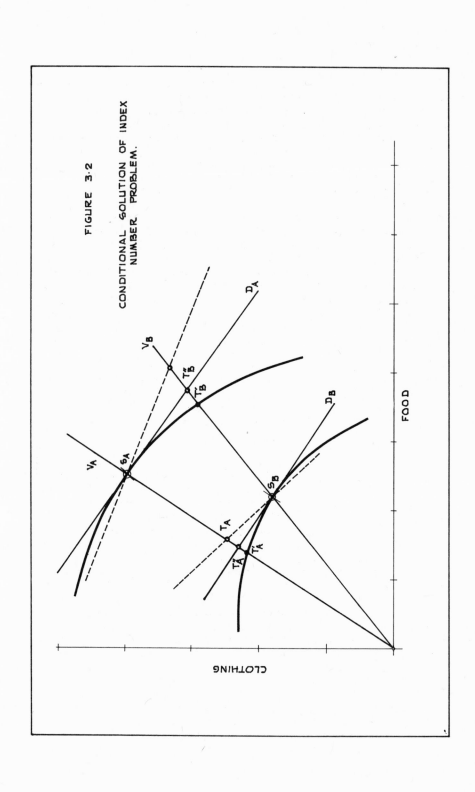

FIGURE 3·2

CONDITIONAL SOLUTION OF INDEX
NUMBER PROBLEM.

periods. That is, this is the ratio defined by the point on the product mix ray where it intersects the prices of A divided by the actual B relative quantities to which the A prices are also applied. In other words, a closer approximation to the true capacity to produce the B mix is given by using the A prices.

Similar reasoning shows that the B prices give a better measure of the true change in the capacity to produce the A product mix.

NOTES

(1) Not on a regular basis at any rate. Occasionally, as in a speech of Party Secretary Brezhenev in March 1971, the absolute figures are reported for certain aggregates - ND and total (sovokupnaia) social product, in this case (Pravda, March 31, 1971, p. 4).

(2) Differences between the levels of the two income measures, and hence in their year-to-year changes, are due to the amount of double counting which is a function of organizational subordination and structure. If vertical integration increases, all other things equal, ND will remain constant while GSP will rise.

(3) We note that if the comparisons of Nash can be taken as representative of the U.S./USSR urban relationship generally, even allowing a very large error, a comparison with calculations of Yasushi Toda for the late Tsarist period shows a sharp relative deterioration for the urban Russian consumer over the period 1913-1966. Toda estimates the relative per capita consumption of the Russian city dweller as 36-63% of his U.S. counterpart, depending on assumptions (Toda, p. 25). This comparison, while interesting, also fails to consider the change in population composition and so cannot be used for nationwide inferences.

(4) The idea of using the average of the rates of growth observed in successive periods, each of which is measured in terms of one of the sets of prices relevant to that period is not new, Gregory Grossman having suggested such a procedure in his 1953 article (1953, pp. 3-5). Grossman's discussion is similar in spirit to the presentation here, both of them attempting to characterize some abstract or pure ability of an economy to grow, rather than the growth with respect to some given set of circumstances. Grossman terms this rate the "own rate of growth" of an economy. His solution, however, stopped short of the choice of initial or end-year price weights, a choice that can now be made with the help of the Bergson presentation (1961).

(5) In this estimate we are observing the same principles as in our choice of a single estimate for total growth throughout the period, i.e., measuring the 1928-37 output growth in terms of 1937 prices, which give the best measure of the change in ability to produce the 1928 mix, and the 1937-55 growth in 1950 prices, which give the best measure of change in ability to produce the 1937 mix. Use of 1928 prices to measure change (or Bergson's "composite" series) would, naturally, show considerably higher growth. (Basic data from Bergson, 1961, p. 271.)

4 Spatial Efficiency

In this and the next three chapters we turn to the study of economic efficiency under Soviet socialism. We will treat four important functional or substantive aspects of efficiency: spatial decisions and relations, efficiency in agriculture, efficiency in industry, and the potential efficiency or inefficiency of the price mechanism.

We will break down the analysis of spatial efficiency into the following questions:

Was the activity level of the transport sector excessive in relation to total social cost minimization? If so,

a) was it due to poor distribution and shipping patterns, or

b) was it due to the location pattern?

Were given transport activity levels achieved at minimum cost?

Was location efficient? If not,

Were there justifiable political-military reasons for selecting the economically inefficient location strategy actually chosen? Whether or not there were,

Were decisions efficient subject to political-military constraints as perceived by the decision makers (whether explicitly formulated or not)?

To answer these questions we undertake an analysis of transportation efficiency in the first section of this chapter and then we analyze location patterns.

TRANSPORTATION EFFICIENCY

Between 1927 and 1940 Soviet transport utilization as measured by rail ton-mileage rose by 408% while tonnage originated increased by

336% (Hunter, pp. 345-7). Was this growth in utilization of railways (which accounted for around 80% of total transport ton-mileage during the period) a necessary result of the increase in the pace of development during the first three five-year plans, or did it also reflect an irrational demand for transportation caused by poor marketing, irrational formulation of product mix, and regional misallocation of investment? This question can be analyzed through an examination of the impact of the hydraulic cement industry's operations on the demand for transportation. This industry is chosen for analysis because of 1) its size and rate of growth (output grew by 207% between 1928 and 1940 vs., for example, 282% for rolled steel); 2) its relatively simple cost structure and limited opportunities for economies of scale; 3) the widespread distribution of raw materials, resulting in small regional variations in production cost; and 4) the homogeneity of use of cement - as an input for construction - which makes the demand for it easier to anticipate than is the demand for other industrial materials, and simplifies the problem of location and facilitates retrospective analysis.

In spite of the factors conducive to a market-oriented location, the length of haul in the 1930s was, in most years, about three or more times as long as it had been in 1912, as is shown in Table 4.1, and transportation costs averaged about 50% of the total delivered cost of cement.

Three potential sources of short-run spatial inefficiency in the cement industry may be distinguished. These are:

1) Inefficient utilization of various modes of transport for a given volume of cement. This may arise from:

   a) selection of the wrong mode of transport between certain origins and destinations;

   b) imperfect transport patterns, i.e., incorrect linking of various producers and users within modes of transport.

2) Inefficient allocation of production targets among plants, possibly resulting in lower industry average production costs, but also in higher average delivered costs than necessary.

3) A poor product mix, heavily weighted by low-strength cements necessitating the transport of greater tonnages to achieve given concrete strength requirements.

We will measure the first and third kinds of inefficiency. For the first, we first analyze the proportions of total cement haulage by each mode of transport, and then test the efficiency of the use of the routes actually employed. The latter is based in part on a linear programming model which was used to determine the optimal transport pattern, which was then compared with the actual pattern. The deviation between the two was not very serious.

A priori there are many reasons to expect that prewar transport patterns were inefficient. First, we know that the period was characterized by extreme pressures and shortages. A second reason is

TABLE 4.1. Average Length of Cement Haul for Selected Years and Averages for Individual Modes of Transport (kilometers)

(1)	(2)	(3)	(4)	(5)	(6)	(7)
			Length of Cement Haul by Individual Modes			
Year	Adjusted All-Mode Average	All-Mode Average Given in Sources	Rail	Rail Tonnage as Percent of Total Tonnage	Water	Movements Involving Rail & Water
1912	450	450				
1924/25	935	935				
1927/28	750	733	599			
1931	800	733	720			
1932	1,200	1,136	1,100			
1933	1,800	1,742	1,310	(89.3)	5,362	
1934	1,750	1,684	1,112	(81.0)	3,469	7,799
1935 (2nd half)	807	733	748	(89.3)	895	1,502
1936 (1st half)	1,150	1,040	1,069	(85.8)	611	2,159
1937	1,090	1,019	977			
1939	1,325		1,353	(94.4)	572	
1950	680	680				
1955	554	554				
1957	530	530				
1968	477					

Sources: Various Soviet industry and planning journals and official rail statistics as described in Abouchar (1971) and Abouchar (1976).

that Russian observers themselves often complained (and continue to do so today) that the cement industry was typified by inefficient haulage operations. Crosshauls are frequently adduced as evidence of this inefficiency, and a more rational scheme for the supply relations of a few origins and destinations is often presented. The distribution of traffic between modes is sometimes criticized as well. Also, the industry's organizational development at the time lacked a firm basis and clear guiding principles, so that disorganized distribution activities might be expected. Other less direct reasons for expecting inefficient transport operations are the railway rate and cement pricing policies at this time. How justified are our expectations?

Efficiency of the Intermodal Split

From time to time in Soviet periodicals greater use of river and of joint rail/river transport has been urged for the haulage of a great many commodities. Holland Hunter describes the often justified reluctance of customers to use river transport for their goods; problems arise in the limited navigable year of most rivers, the need to maintain larger stocks, the damage to metals inflicted by river moisture, and the reloading cost of joint haulage (Hunter, pp. 156-160). These or similar objections are also relevant, on many routes, to river transport of cement, a mode which, it is often urged, should take a greater share of cement traffic. (1)

Analysis of the routes actually used in 1936, however, indicates that the modal distribution was rational. Cement was shipped by water over many Black Sea routes, which were much shorter and had appreciably lower costs per kilometer than the corresponding rail routes. The other major water routes were from Vol'sk down the Volga to Moscow and from Novorossiisk to Leningrad by a combination of the river Dnepr and railway. These routes were, respectively, 20% and 3% lower, in terms of social costs, than the all-rail routes, all things considered. Water shipment was limited to such advantageous routes for the most part, and the use of water routes for other shipments would not have represented a saving over rail for any or all of the following reasons: water routes were much longer than the corresponding rail routes, obviating in part the lower cost per kilometer by river; spoilage was greater by water; combined rail/water shipments required extra loading costs, offsetting part of the advantage of the water portion of the journey; bags or barrels were required to prevent hydration en route.

Crosshauls and Other Inefficiencies

Next we consider the rationality of use patterns within specific modes of transport, especially the railways. Were needlessly long hauls used? Were there wasteful crosshauls: the repeated animadversions and exhortations of Soviet writers on the subject of transportation operations in the cement industry suggest that this was the case. For example, Brodskii, citing a wasteful crosshaul between Moscow and cities down the Volga, criticizes the industry's distribution apparatus (1935, p. 12). The following year two observers point to the substantial reduction in the average haul of cement between 1934 and 1935 as evidence of more rational marketing and distribution methods in 1935. This reduction in average haul is seen in Table 4.1 to be dramatic indeed - about 50% from the 1934 level. However, to interpret the average length of haul as a direct reflection of the efficiency of distribution requires, among other things, constant regional production and consumption patterns and, to be sure, Smurov and Slivitskii do maintain that "there were really no serious changes in the geography of the cement industry" (Smurov and Slivitskii, 1936, p. 44). But this is not true: the proportion of national cement consumption accounted for by East Siberia and the Far East fell by about two-thirds - from 10.3% to 3.6% - between 1934 and 1935, reducing the average haul of cement by about 550 kilometers. It then more than doubled to 7.7% in 1936 and the average haul rose in consequence.

The great drop in the average haul of cement between 1934 and 1935 represents a change in consumption patterns rather than improvement in the efficiency of distribution as claimed by Smurov and Slivitskii. However, this in itself does not mean that distribution may not have been inefficient in all years. The question of the efficiency of distribution may be resolved, however, by means of a linear program solution through which the actual and optimal patterns of distribution, given the existing structure of consumption and production, can be compared.

A linear programming analysis of the transport patterns of the first half of 1936 showed that they were relatively rational, the divergence between actual and optimal patterns being less than 7%. The reliability of this rather surprising conclusion is supported by the unambiguity of the input data for the analysis - there were no significant problems in determining actual haulage distances between producing and consuming regions and the regionalization used was finely detailed; for example, Ukraine and Crimea were divided into seven regions as was the industrial center around Moscow. The results just cited for 1936 are reinforced by less formal calculations for 1939 which, together with the absence of strong contrary evidence (the Smurov-Slivitskii reasoning itself having no firm basis), suggest that distribution operations were efficient throughout the prewar period.

To state what we have established so far: The huge increases in transport utilization in general far exceeded the growth of the economy, and the growth of cement traffic in particular was far greater than the increase in production. But the increases were not due to inefficient transport utilization, and we have found no evidence of inefficient transport operations arising in other sources which would not show up in growth of transport output; to be precise, the modal split was efficient, and the intra-railroad network plan was close to the linear program solution. The tremendous increase in cement transportation - both ton-kilometers and the average length of haul - had their genesis elsewhere: the long average haul in a pattern of new capacity

location and cement utilization which was different from the historical
pattern and which, moreover, was not efficient (as we see below); the
sharp increase in ton-kilometers had its origin in this location pattern
and partly in the product characteristics of the industry with too much
low-strength cement being produced, requiring more transport per ton
of finished concrete of specified strength.

The analysis of the efficiency of transportation, and of the interplay
between transportation and location can be shown with production
diagrams. Figure 4.1 shows a hypothetical production expansion path.
Physical capital, assumed to be measurable in some units, is measured
on the vertical axis, and transportation inputs, in ton-kilometers, say,
on the horizontal. Any combination of the two will be associated with
some output level, and that output level can also be attained with
different combinations of transport and cement production capital. The
optimal output is determined by the tangency of the price line, PP,
which shows true relative costs, to the producer (which we might regard
as private costs), and the production isoquant. Essentially, what is
being shown above, in combination with the analysis of location to
follow, is that the industry did not produce at a point of tangency; this
means that with the same total resource input, a higher quantity could
have been produced or, conversely, that the same quantity could have
been produced with a smaller resource input.

Before leaving our analysis of transportation, we must also ask
whether, whatever the efficiency or inefficiency of the ton-kilo-
meterage actually used by the industry, it was attained at minimum
social cost. Again, we may think in terms of production isoquants, two
factors, capital and labor, plotted on the two axes, and any isoquant
indicating the production of ton-kilometers. What can be said about
this aspect of cost minimization?

There is really no study which would enable us to answer this
question. On the other hand, it seems reasonable that given the facts
that transport scheduling was rational, so that the level of ton-
kilometers of output was justified for the given location variant, and
that workers everywhere were concerned with cost minimization to
achieve given output levels as the Stakhanov movement spread during
the 1930s, we would probably be justified in believing that the total
output of ton-kilometers that was produced was in fact produced at
minimum cost. When studying any particular industry it is usually a
much more difficult question to ask whether the output level was
rational and as we have seen, the ton-kilometers actually performed in
the prewar period did constitute an efficient activity level given the
existing location variant which, we will see below, was inefficient.

What of the postwar period? For this we turn to the study of
Norman Kaplan which showed that the average output-factor ratios
(capital and labor) grew steadily through 1963. The link relatives for
four sub-periods (the ratios of the growth in output to the growth in
capital stock and to the growth in labor input) were as shown in Table
4.2.

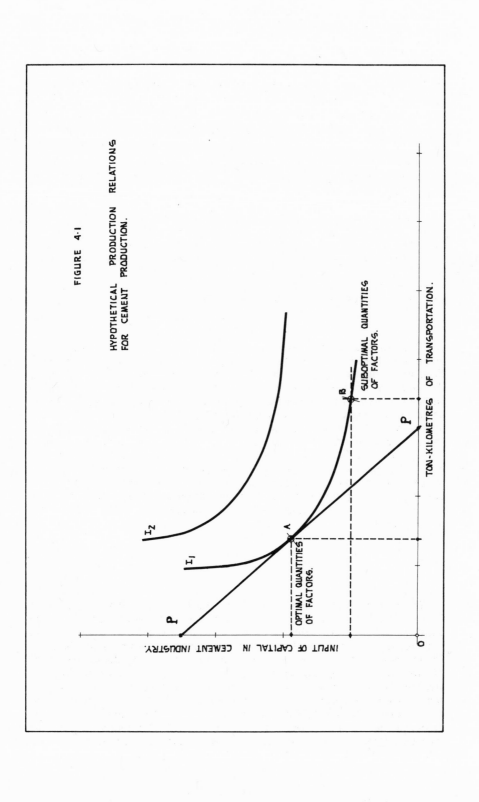

FIGURE 4·1

HYPOTHETICAL   PRODUCTION   RELATIONS
FOR   CEMENT   PRODUCTION.

INPUT OF CAPITAL IN CEMENT INDUSTRY.

I_2

I_1

P

P

A

B

OPTIMAL QUANTITIES
OF FACTORS.

SUBOPTIMAL QUANTITIES
OF FACTORS.

TON-KILOMETRES OF TRANSPORTATION.

O

TABLE 4.2.   Indexes of Output Growth in Relation to Growth of
             Factor Inputs, 1928-1963, and Selected Sub-periods

	Output/ Capital	Output/ Labor
1928-1963	1.83	3.76
1928-1940	1.18	1.28
1940-1951	1.06	1.15
1951-1958	1.40	1.78
1958-1963	1.03	1.44

Source: Calculated from Kaplan (1967).

To show that these ratios were growing over time, of course, is no
guarantee that they might not have grown still faster. For example,
even granting that activity levels were on production isoquants before
the war, as we have argued, it is conceivable that the technological
potentials grew faster than the output levels following the war. Looked
at from the viewpoint of production possibilities schedules one could
hypothesize that while the prewar output level was on the production
frontier, the frontier shifted more rapidly than the production point
moved from the origin; production came to take place at an interior, or
inefficient point. This is always a possibility, but there does not seem
to be any reason to expect things to have developed in this way.
Barring firm arguments for such expectations, it seems reasonable to
conclude that the efficiency of prewar transport use continued into the
postwar period.

LOCATION

There are today many interesting questions of location strategy.
Controversy with the Chinese provides political motivation for faster
build-up of Eastern Siberia and the Far East; the potential for
petroleum exports, as well as the future need to ensure a supply of oil
for the Soviet Union's own use, provide an impetus for the development
of the northern regions of Siberia.   But while decisions on location
strategy remain urgent, it is probably true that the location decisions in
the 1930s were relatively more consequential than those being made
today, even though today's decisions may involve absolutely larger
resource quantities.   Accordingly, it is the efficiency of prewar
location strategy and tactics that we must analyze following the
scheme presented in the introduction to this chapter.

Was Prewar Location Efficient?

The major evidence on overall prewar locational efficiency is in the study by Ivan Koropeckyj (1971) which examined Soviet location policies in relation to the Ukrainian Republic. Koropeckyj looked at the breakdown of total investment in the entire economy and in industry during the first two five-year plans between Ukraine and the total USSR. He also considered the distribution of investment for 15 important industries. These distributions were evaluated from the viewpoint of the incremental capital output ratio (ICOR). If we leave aside political concerns for the moment, concentrate on economic efficiency and also neglect transport considerations, efficiency in location requires that investment be channeled into regions on the basis of the ICOR, with investment in each region continued up to the point where the ICOR is equal in all regions and in all industries. Such an evaluation requires knowledge of the effect of investment on a local ICOR, which may be to raise or lower the ratio of the target industry as well as on the supplier and client industries. This information is not available for the Soviet Union and in fact would be unlikely to be available for any other country either. Thus all we can say is, roughly, that relatively more investment should go to Ukraine than to other regions, since a ruble of investment there would typically generate a larger volume of output in that republic. But mere knowledge of the ICOR is not enough to tell us how much more intense investment should have been from an efficiency standpoint, since we do not know how much investment would have been necessary to equalize the ICOR in all regions. The actual broad investment picture is shown in Table 4.3.

One possible lead to analyzing this issue would be to compare total investment allocation during the period to the capital stock in place on the eve of the plan. Koropeckyj shows that in 1928 Ukraine accounted for 21.1% of total productive fixed capital stock of large-scale industry (1971, p. 22). Since this capital was more productive, it should have increased faster, which would indicate that a higher percentage of new investment should have gone to Ukraine than elsewhere although, as Table 4.3 shows, it was slightly lower in both the first and second five-year plans. In addition, Ukraine was itself a major population center, and also had excellent rail connections to other heavily populated areas west of the Urals, so that even with equal ICORs greater investment would be indicated for Ukraine, on efficiency grounds. Considering this together with the likelihood that diseconomies would not begin to arise in Ukraine for a considerable time, and assuming that investment in newer regions would start to reduce their ICORs straightaway, still suggests that investment in the Ukraine on the order of 25% of total investment might have been the most efficient course to follow. This suggests therefore that investment during these two five-year plans was not allocated efficiently among regions.

This hypothesis is further corroborated by Koropeckyj's data on the inter-industrial distribution of investment. He shows that the industries with the lowest ICOR in Ukraine were not favored in investment. All other things being equal we should expect to find, if investment were

TABLE 4.3.   Investment in Ukraine and in all USSR under First
and Second Five-Year Plans

	Ukraine	USSR	Ukraine/ USSR (%)
	millions of rubles		
Total National Econony			
First FYP	1,243	6,716	18.5
Second FYP	2,521	15,170	16.8
Industry			
First FYP	596	2,897	20.6
Second FYP	1,178	6,377	18.5
Industry as % of Total National Economy			
First FYP	48	43	
Second FYP	47	42	

Source: Koropeckyj (1971), p. 16.

being allocated on the basis of efficiency considerations, that the
capital stock would increase relatively faster in Ukraine for those
industries which have lowest ICOR. From Koropeckyj's data (p. 83), we
can calculate a rank correlation coefficient of .3.

The foregoing indications, while not conclusive, strongly suggest
that investment was not allocated inter-regionally in the most efficient
manner.   However, this in itself may not be a cause for serious
objection to Soviet policy since, as we have stressed repeatedly, there
may have been considerations other than efficiency. For the 1930s the
main "non-economic" consideration was probably military security,
although some observers of Soviet policy have held that it was
conditioned also by the desire to achieve some greater equality in inter-
regional industrialization levels and growth rates, which would also
serve the purpose of minimizing secessionist moves by strong ethnic
groups. Koropeckyj himself does not speculate on the motives, devoting
his analysis only to the question of whether the distribution of
investment was or was not economically efficient and concluding that
"there should be not the slightest doubt that a substantially larger share
of total investment in the USSR should have been allocated to the
development of Ukrainian industry during the first two Five-Year Plans
than actually was the case" (p. 50).

POLITICAL-MINISTRY JUSTIFICATION FOR
THE DISTRIBUTION OF INVESTMENT

The major shift in the location of industry during the first two five-year plans was toward the east - the Ural Mountains and beyond. Some plants were actually dismantled and relocated there and a huge amount of a new industrial investment was directed to that vast region. The main reason for this shift in industrial capital to regions with higher ICOR, and from which transportation communications to the traditional western regions are longer, was uncertainty and the suspicion that war would break out with Germany. The major single investment project during this time was the UKK (Ural-Kuznetsk Kombinat), which accounted for almost 25% of total investment in industry in the first five-year plan and nearly 30% in the second five-year plan. During these years it was expected to increase its share of total ferrous metals production from 15% in 1927-28 to 32% in 1937 (Holzman, 1962, p. 382), the 1937 activity level, of course, comprising a share of a much much larger national output, steel production quadrupling over this period (Promyshlennost' 1964, pp. 170-71). The UKK project was a huge venture combining coal and steel deposits 2,400 kilometers apart, to be joined by a railroad line, part of which had to be built from scratch, with a shuttle rail service carrying coal to the Urals and iron ore to the Kuznetsk coal basin in Western Siberia.

The strategic considerations were that in case of war, it would be necessary to maintain a steel industry which, given the vulnerability of the Ukraine, must be located further west beyond the reaches of possible advance by the German armies. The project, it should be stressed, was a very costly one; the relative costs of production were calculated to be lower than in the traditional Ukrainian production centers, but these calculations are based on an understated railroad cost, which in turn probably represents the attempt to make this political decision appear economically palatable. In addition, the lower calculated cost failed to take account of the longer immobilization of capital investment in steel production and related facilities than would have been necessary for expansion in Ukraine. Holzman concludes that the decision would probably have been necessary eventually from an economic efficiency point of view in any case, since one day steel expansion in Ukraine would have to stop or slow down because of the necessary recourse to high cost resources, but that it was premature. Strategic considerations, however, would justify it.

Following the war, many Russian writers pointed to this project in self-congratulatory enthusiasm as an example of the foresight and wisdom that the socialist planned economy could muster, a conclusion seriously challenged by the major Western analyst of the Soviet steel industry, Gardner Clark (1956), who has argued that invocation of military-strategic needs, in fact, played little explicit role in the decision. Whether it hovered in the background of Soviet thinking as an important consideration, or was recognized but simply not believed deserving of unnecessary repetition, is difficult to evaluate. Clark argues that it would be difficult to reconcile any such thesis with the unabated bloodletting in the military officer corps, which accompanied Stalin's purges, an argument which it is hard to challenge. In addition, one must be suspicious even of the Soviet argument following the war that the UKK enabled the Soviet Union to resist, repel, and conquer the German armies. This argument overlooks the great contribution made to the Soviet war effort by United States military assistance in the form of lend-lease and direct aid. Nevertheless, the project did enable the Soviet Union to maintain steel production throughout the war, which certainly must have contributed to the war effort, even if it was not the only source of supply of military matériel.

It seems fair to say, then, that no explicit and consistent military/strategic considerations informed the decision to shift the industrial base of the economy; and even if such considerations, unspoken rather than explicit, did condition the location policy of the political leadership, it would remain questionable whether the shift would in any event have been enough to withstand the German invasion. Information is incomplete, however, so that the canons of scholarship dictate that we suspend final judgment and turn instead to the question whether, since a geographical shift was taking place - whether for reasons of military strategy or as an attempt to reduce the economic power of one important constituent people, the Ukrainians - it was done in the most efficient way possible.

EFFICIENCY OF INVESTMENT ALLOCATION SUBJECT TO NON-ECONOMIC CONSTRAINTS

Even if one accepts the argument that it would be desirable to disperse industrial location for non-economic reasons, it remains to be asked whether the overall investment program, subject to this constraint, was efficient. As we will see, some very serious errors were committed.

Our analysis will be based on the cement industry. Cement production technology did not dictate a concentrated industry. Raw materials of comparable quality were found extensively in the USSR, holding down cost variation of the regional production. And scale economies are modest in comparison with high real transport costs in any event. Therefore, an efficient location pattern for this industry is one which approximates the geographical demand pattern, and a widely dispersed industry should be expected. Did the Russians plan new capacity consistently with this optimal location pattern?

Table 4.4 shows the changes in regional shares in consumption and production between 1913 and 1940. Information on consumption is less easily available than that on production and can be given for only a few years. The data shown refer to total hydraulic cement production and consumption. Local production of cement types, such as portland-slag or portland-pozzolan blends, was dictated by raw materials' availability, the slag blends accompanying steel production, and the pozzolans being

TABLE 4.4.　Regional Production and Consumption of Hydraulic Cements in Thirteen Regions - Selected Years
(1. Thousands of tons　　2. Percentage of total)

Region		Production 1913	1929/30	1932	1936 (first half)	1936	1937	1940	Consumption 1913	1929/30	1936 (first half)	1936	1940
North	1.	—	—	—	—	—	—	—	24	60	9	20	91
	2.	0.0	0.0	0.0	0.0	0.0	0.0	0.0	1.5	1.7	0.3	0.3	1.7
Northwest	1.	102	164	131	78	165	168	95	149	303	205	456	551
	2.	6.3	4.7	3.8	2.9	2.8	3.1	1.7	9.2	8.6	7.9	7.9	10.5
Center, West and Central Black Earth	1.	307	801	556	490	1071	1215	1144	507	875	878	1953	1085
	2.	19.0	23.1	16.0	18.4	18.2	22.3	20.5	34.5	24.8	33.8	33.8	20.6
Volga	1.	326	641	569	288	706	522	524	95	218	117	260	319
	2.	20.2	18.5	16.4	10.8	11.9	9.6	9.4	5.9	6.2	4.5	4.5	6.1
North Caucasus	1.	394	882	1050	589	1246	1022	962	152	205	198	440	523
	2.	24.4	25.5	30.2	22.1	21.0	18.7	17.2	9.4	5.8	7.6	7.6	9.9
Urals	1.	63	179	193	142	406	375	345	69	339	165	367	427
	2.	3.9	5.2	5.5	5.3	6.8	6.9	6.2	4.3	9.6	6.3	6.3	8.1
West Siberia	1.		77	131	141	283	242	263		118	53	118	182
	2.		2.2	3.8	5.3	4.8	4.4	4.7		3.3	2.0	2.0	3.5
East Siberia	1.	60	—	—	—	—	—	—	113	30	57	127	72
	2.	3.7	0.0	0.0	0.0	0.0	0.0	0.0	7.0	0.9	2.2	2.2	1.4
Far East	1.		40	36	59	149	164	234		103	139	309	458
	2.		1.2	1.0	2.2	2.5	3.0	4.2		2.9	5.3	5.3	8.7
Central Asia-Kazakh SSR	1.	3	27	69	49	153	128	267	14	234	98	218	267
	2.	0.2	0.8	2.0	1.8	2.6	2.3	4.8	0.9	6.6	3.8	3.8	5.1
Transcaucasia	1.	47	72	208	165	330	291	326	105	180	188	418	421
	2.	2.9	2.1	6.0	6.2	5.6	5.3	5.8	6.5	5.1	7.2	7.2	8.0
Ukraine	1.	314	580	535	598	1287	1220	1218	360	800	434	965	750
	2.	19.4	16.7	15.4	22.5	21.8	22.4	21.8	22.3	22.7	16.7	16.7	14.2
Belorussian SSR	1.	—	—	—	61	120	107	200	26	59	58	129	122
	2.	0.0	0.0	0.0	2.3	2.0	2.0	3.6	1.6	1.7	2.2	2.2	2.3
Total (thousands of tons)		1616	3463	3478	2660	5916	5454	5578	1616	3524	2599	5780	5268

1940 information from Z. I. Loginov, Tsem. prom. SSSR (Moscow, Gosplanizdat, 1960), pp. 134-135. Loginov combines Belorussian consumption with that of the Baltic republics. Estimate given here is based on 1960 proportions in E. G. Gutsev, "Perevozka mineral'nykh stroitel'nykh materialov," Chapter II in E. G. Gutsev et al., Ratsionalizatsiia perevozok massovykh gruzov v BSSR, Izdatel'stvo Akademii Nauk BSSR, 1960.
1937 data from Promyshlennost' 1957, p. 279.
1936 production data from Brodskii 1938, p. 11.
1936 first half production and consumption from Brodskii 1937a. Brodskii does not give consumption for 1936 as a whole. The full-year basis estimates given here preserve the relative half-year consumption shares, while the ratio between the full-year estimate of consumption and the annual production volume maintains the relationship existing between Brodskii's first-half data.
It should be noted that production in 1936 rose sharply from the previous year largely because of an NKTP Bureau of Standardization Decree of March 1936 permitting the addition of hydraulic additives to portland cement without changing its designation (see Chapter II, section A.1). The resulting product appears not to have been successful and to have led to a cutback in blending in 1937. In that year with portland-slag and pozzolan production almost equal to that of 1936, there was a reduction of about 12 percent in portland production at the same time that kiln productivity was almost unchanged (533 kilograms of klinker per day per cubic meter of kiln volume in 1936 vs. 531 in 1937). E. S. Shatalov, "Zadachi tsementnoi promyshlennosti," Ts. (1938), p. 10. 1932 data from Promyshlennost' 1957, p. 279.
1929/30 information from "Novye metody sostavleniia balansa stroitel'nykh materialov i ikh raspredeleniia mezhdu stroiiashchimi oranizatsiiami," NS (1930), No. 7-8, p. 274. Siberian information, there aggregated, here is divided between Western and Eastern Siberia in accordance with trends since 1927/28 (NKPS, Materialy po statistike putei soobshcheniia, Vyp. 108, Svodnaia statistika perevozok po zheleznym dorogam za 1927/28 operats. god, Tom II, Transpechat', 1930), and 1933 (Brodskii 1935a).
1913 information from V. Shneider and G. Brodskii, "Itogi i perspektivy razmeshecheniia tsementnoi promyshlennost," PKh (1939), No. 2. The authors left undistributed 10 percent of total production and 23 percent of total consumption. These quantities have been distributed here in proportion to the balances, except for Northern and Belorussian consumption, which has been based on the trends, and the Central industrial regions, which have been lowered slightly to allow for the consumption of the two aforementioned regions.

TABLE 4.5. Analysis of Delivered Costs of Cement in 1940

| | Costs under Actual Production Location Pattern | | | | | | Costs under Alternative Production Location Pattern | | | | |
Region	(1) Production (000 tons)	(2) Production Cost per Ton (portland) (rubles)	(3) Adjusted Average Cost (rubles)	(4) Total Production Cost (000 rubles) (col. 1 × col. 3)	(5) Tonnage to Be Produced for Designated Consuming Region (000 tons)	Consuming Region	(6) Cost of Production (000 rubles) (col. 5 × col. 3)	(7) Estimated Average Length of Haul to Supply Designated Consuming Region (km.)	(8) Average Rail Cost per Ton (rubles) (col. 7 × 1.2 k.)	(9) Total Rail Cost to Supply Designated Consuming Region (000 rubles) (col. 5 × col. 8)	(10) Total Production + Transport Cost to Supply Designated Consuming Region (000 rubles) (col. 6 × col. 9)
North	—		48.0	—	91	North[a]	2,375.1	1,100	13.31	1,211.2	3,586.3
Northwest	95	42.0	42.0	3,985.2		Center West, and Central					
Center, West, and Central											
Black Earth	1,144	28.0	26.1	29,858.4	1,085	Black Earth	28,318.5	190	2.30	2,495.5	30,814.0
Volga	524	25.8	24.6	12,890.4	319	Volga	7,847.4	750	9.08	2,896.5	10,743.9
North Caucasus	962	25.8	25.0	24,050.0	523	North Caucasus	13,075.0	450	5.44	2,845.1	15,920.1
Urals	345	29.1	22.3	7,693.5	427	Urals	9,522.1	375	4.54	1,938.6	11,460.7
West Siberia	263	29.1	22.0	5,786.0	182	West Siberia	4,004.0	275	3.33	606.1	4,610.1
East Siberia	—	—	53.0	—	72	East Siberia	3,816.0	500	6.05	435.6	4,251.6
Far East	234	51.7	51.7	12,097.8	458	Far East	23,678.6	350	4.24	1,941.9	25,620.5
Central Asia-						Central Asia -					
KSSR	267	45.2	42.1	11,240.7	267	KSSR	11,240.7	400	4.84	1,292.3	12,533.0
Transcaucasia	326	29.1	27.4	8,932.4	421	Transcaucasia	11,535.4	250	3.02	1,271.4	12,806.8
Ukraine	908	22.6	17.6	15,980.8	750	Ukraine	13,200.0	215	2.60	1,950.0	15,150.0
Belorussian SSR	200	29.1	29.1	5,820.0	122	Belorussian SSR	3,550.2	342	4.14	505.1	4,055.3
					551	Northwest[b]	16,034.1	788	9.53	5,251.0	21,285.1
Total	5,268			138,335.2	5,268		148,197.1			24,630.3	172,837.4

	Costs under Actual Production Location Pattern	Costs under Alternative Production Location Pattern
Total production cost	138,335.2	148,197.1
Total carrying cost	93,019.6	24,630.3
Total handling cost	8,951.4	8,428.8
Total of production, carrying, and handling costs	230,306.2	181,256.2
Packaging costs	30,000.0	
Dust loss factor adjustment	−11,421.5	−16,211.0
Total delivered cost under this location variant	248,884.7	165,045.2

[a] Supplied from Center under alternative variant.
[b] Supplied from Belorussian SSR under alternative variant.

located primarily in southern European Russia (Volga, Northern Caucasus, and Transcaucasus) and Central Asia.

Portland cement blended with pozzolanic additives did have an advantage over straight portland in certain types of structures, which may have necessitated the shipment of blends even to regions which were cement-surplus areas when all types were considered together. This in turn would have raised the calculated average length of haul. However, all major regions had their own source of blended portland, the major exceptions being Leningrad and the Far East. But the need for blends should not be overstressed; the main variable was production cost, and the special characteristic of lower heat of hydration of pozzolan was rarely taken into account in the Soviet journals of the pre-war period. (2)

That the Soviet cement industry was unsatisfactorily located in the 1930s came to be recognized and discussed only after 1937 - that is, only after the end of the second five-year plan. Only rarely did the industry's observers correctly point to the very long average haul, shown in Table 4.1, as evidence of this inefficient location; most observers pointed to the long average haul as evidence of inefficient marketing which, as we have seen, is an incorrect view. Still other writers deny the validity of a comparison between the values of this measure in the 1930s and in the pre-revolutionary period, because of the radically altered demand patterns. But to the last objection may be counterposed the argument that any capacity distribution is supposed to represent the adjustments required by the demand pattern which has developed and, because cement production is not seriously restricted by raw materials location or scale economies, there is nothing to keep these adjustments from being easily made. An average haul which for ten years remained two to four times longer than that previously existing, while production increased by about 250% as compared with the Tsarist period, strongly suggests that these adjustments were not being made.

The consumption figures in Table 4.4 reflect what actually occurred. Independent analysis of the expectations for cement consumption, which might be inferred from the first and second five-year plans, supports the view that heavy consumption should have been foreseen in the east (western and eastern Siberia, and the Far East), which were to account for 12.3% of total investment under the second plan (Abouchar, 1971, p. 52). In other words, the total of 13.6% of actual consumption in these regions in 1940 should not be considered as unexpected or as the result of the prior location there of cement capacity.

Clearly, the actual distribution of production and consumption represented a major shift from the Tsarist period. The consumption pattern itself appeared to reflect the changing location of all industry and the needs for cement to achieve this new spatial pattern. It is to the analysis of the efficiency of the production pattern which developed that we now turn. Did this pattern minimize total delivered costs?

Table 4.5 provides the basic data required for the analysis. We consider prewar boundaries and the same regionalization used in Table 4.4. Columns 1-4 relate to the actual production pattern, while columns 5-10 relate to the cost of an alternative pattern. Column 1 gives the regional production level in 1940 as shown in Table 4.4, except that since consumption (5,268,000 tons) fell short of production (5,578,000 tons), we have reduced production by 310,000 tons. Column 2 gives regional mill prices for grade 00 portland. These prices are believed to accurately reflect the cost of this grade portland in the various regions.

Column 3 represents an attempt to estimate average regional production cost based on the 1932-35 price list which took effect in 1932. This adjustment takes account of each region's product mix and makes use of the regional distribution of portland-slag and pozzolan production. The costs of these cements were estimated by adding to the cost of the portland component, which is 50% for pozzolan and 20% for portland-slag, the cost of processing and grinding the hydraulic additive. This cost for each of these additives was estimated to be 60% of the production cost of portland cement. The resulting costs estimated for pozzolan and portland-slag are 80% and 68% respectively, of the cost grade 00 portland. These ratios are somewhat lower than the relative mill prices as compared with portland. Since slag is most important in Ukraine and pozzolans are most important in the west, this is a conservative approach. It helps to justify the increased production that developed in these regions during the decade, which then required very long hauls for shipment to the east.

Finally, column 4 gives the cost of producing in each region the amount that actually was produced. The entries in this column are the product of the entries in columns 1 and 3. The total cost of producing by this regional production plan is 138.3 million rubles.

Next we must calculate the delivery costs incurred for this volume. Earlier, an estimate of 1.2 kopecks was developed as the total ton-kilometer social cost of cement transportation in 1932 for the haul itself (Abouchar, 1971, Ch. II). It was reasoned that the approximate constancy of the unit charge imposed by the new rate structure in 1939 was characteristic of the real cost structure for hauling cement earlier in the period (this cost does not include the loading and unloading cost, which must be added). We can now multiply this cost by the number of rail-ton kilometers recorded for 1940 in order to get a total rail transport cost and add to it the water transport cost.

The input coefficient for physical transport for 1940 is not known. It is known for 1939, however, as is the breakdown between water and rail use. This was shown in Table 4.1. From this information and from data available on the cost of shipping by water, it is possible to estimate the total cost of transport in money. Total rail-ton kilometerage will be 6,728 million, which yields a rail-carrying cost of 80.7 rubles (the average cost, including handling or transloading, where necessary, of 1.35 kopecks per ton-kilometer). To this must be added the loading and unloading cost of 4,973,000 tons that went by rail, or 8,951,400 rubles, giving a total production and shipping cost of 230,306,200 rubles, including 138.3 million for production and 92.0 million for transportation.

The cost of an alternative regional location pattern is shown in columns 5-10. Column 5 gives the production required in each region to correspond to the consumption requirements listed in Table 4.4, with the exception that self-sufficiency is not planned for the North or Northwest. Instead, these two regions are to be supplied from the central region and Belorussia respectively. The reason for treating the North in this way is that the delivered cost from the center is less than the estimate of the production cost in the North (48 rubles); the Northwest is handled in this way because Belorussian cement delivered there is somewhat cheaper than that produced in Leningrad and is believed to have been of superior quality. And since cement from the Northwest delivered to Leningard would have exceeded the cost of Belorussian cement, the alternative variant here presented calls for importation from Belorussia. Belorussian cement rather than cement from the Moscow region is proposed here to minimize congestion in the center, although the run from Moscow is somewhat shorter than the haul from Krichev in the Belorussian SSR.

Column 6 contains regional production costs for this alternative locational pattern. The costs used there are those of column 3, which were used in estimating the cost of the actual production pattern. Eastern Siberian cost is estimated to be slightly higher than that in the Far East. The total production cost under this variant is 148.2 million rubles, 7% more than the estimated cost of the actual production pattern. The main differences between the two location patterns are seen to be in lower production levels of Ukraine, the Northern Caucasus, and the Volga region and higher production in the eastern regions in the alternative pattern.

Column 7 contains the estimated average haul within each region. In some of the regions, for example, the center, production originates at several points. Column 8 is the result of multiplying the average hauls of column 7 by 1.2 kopecks. This column gives the estimated average carrying cost per ton of cement shipped within the various regions. Column 9 is the product of multiplying column 8, the average rail cost per ton, by column 5, the relevant tonnage, and gives the transportation cost to supply each region. The total carrying cost is seen to be 24.6 million rubles, a saving of 70% over the actual carrying cost. Finally, column 10 gives the total production plus carrying cost. For the shorter distances involved under this variant, however, all movement could have taken place in bulk, which would have reduced the handling cost to 1.6 rubles per ton. Applying this cost to the 5,268 thousand tons gives a handling cost of 8,428,600 rubles, making a total production and transport cost of 181,256,200 rubles, which in turn represents a saving of 21% over the corresponding cost of the actual pattern.

Still other costs involved in the actual production pattern could have been avoided by the alternatives presented here. In the first place, with the relatively short hauls of the alternative plan, dust loss would have been lower. The average haul implied by the alternative scheme is around 400 kilometers. Since part of the dust loss is incurred in loading and unloading, and only part en route, the saving would not be proportional to the reduction in average haul, which is about 70%. Rather, a reduction in dust loss of around 40% might have been achieved. Therefore, we estimate the average dust loss on bulk shipments as 6% rather than 10%, as in the actual pattern. However, with the shorter hauls all cement may be assumed to have been cheaper to transport in bulk than the 60-70% shipped in bulk in the actual pattern. This loss ratio must therefore be applied to total shipment in the alternative plan, and in the actual pattern the larger loss ratio must be applied to only 60% of the total. The losses calculated in this way are 16.2 million rubles and 11.4 million rubles for the actual and alternative plans respectively and are subtracted from the total delivered costs of the two plans in reverse order. That is, the location variant proposed here would have permitted a saving of 16.2 million rubles, which was the cost of the dust loss in the actual plan, and the actual plan should reflect a saving of the 11.4 million rubles that the alternative plan would involve.

As just noted, it would have been possible to ship all cement in bulk, given the shorter hauls of the alternative plan, except possibly over damp routes; but since the alternative location pattern has been based entirely on rail shipment, instances of loss by moisture would have been quite rare. Therefore, no packing costs need be added to the delivered cost under the alternative plan, and in the actual plan a cost of around 30 million rubles is indicated, on the basis of information presented earlier on packing procedures. This figure reflects the cost of barrels and bags and the use mix. These several cost adjustments are shown in Table 4.5 where the total savings possible through the alternative-location pattern is seen to be 83.8 million rubles - 33% of costs actually incurred!

The savings possible through the new location patterns are substantial. Is there any chance they have been overstated? Possible causes of overstatement in the savings attainable through the alternative-location pattern include underestimation of the intra-regional lengths of haul in column 7, and overestimation of the transport input involved in the actual pattern. Even if the intra-regional hauls had been twice as high as our estimates, however, a substantial saving would still have been achieved - 58 million rubles or 24% of delivered costs. But checks on the accuracy of all estimates of distance, calculated for use in the linear programming exercise mentioned in the section above, indicate that the intra-regional estimates are not likely to be off by more than a few percentage points. By varying the coefficients in column 7, the reader may easily see the effect on total cost of any assumed intra-regional average length of haul. For example, if the Far East intra-regional average haul were assumed to be three times higher, total carrying costs within the Far East under the alternative-location plan would rise by 3.8 million rubles, raising total delivery costs by only 2.3%.

The total social overexpenditure of resources caused by the incorrect location of the industry in 1940 has been estimated at 33%. In addition, the alternative-location pattern here presented envisages more portalnd cement production (in the Far East and Eastern Siberia) and less portland-slag and pozzolan production which, as they actually were produced in the Soviet setting even if not in theory, were inferior in their concrete-making capacity.

During the period of the prewar plan the Soviet cement industry came to be very inefficiently located. The most marked indicator of this inefficiency is the industry's average length of haul, which through most of the period averaged 70% longer than the 1927-28 average and around 200% longer than the average in the pre-revolutionary industry. This increase resulted primarily from the increased demand of the eastern and central Asian regions, where capacity to keep pace was not added.   As we concluded from evidence of contemporary cement consumption projections and capital construction plans, however, these needs ought to have been clearly anticipated and, given the relatively simple nature of cement technology and cost functions, capacity should have been emplaced in these regions.

A precise notion of the cost of the developing locational imbalance was gained through our analysis of 1940. Using estimates of 1932 real social costs for production and transportation, we calculated that 33% of the cost in 1940 represented avoidable waste.   This means an overexpenditure of about 50% over what need have been spent under a regime of economic efficiency.

Three factors seem to have contributed to the poor performance. First, the industry busied itself chiefly with the minimization of production cost rather than total social cost, and new output could generally be secured more rapidly in the west, although not at costs low enough to offset the high transport costs. In the second place, the railroad costs were understated, so that even when the industry may have been interested in minimizing total costs, it probably based its decision on the railroad rates confronting it rather than the true social costs.   There was a major discrepancy between the two before 1939, when the average ton-kilometer costs declined with increasing distances much more than did average costs. Finally, even when observers were concerned with the total picture - that is, with minimization of costs to the economy - they chose the wrong target. When they were concerned about the long average haul, they generally supposed that the solution lay in rationalization of distribution rather than in correction of the locational imbalance, and this attitude undoubtedly begot complacency with respect to the planning of location in the industry. As we have seen through the analysis of transport operations, however, distribution was not the real problem at all.

CONCLUSION

In this chapter we have analyzed one area of decision-making - spatial decisions - from several points of view: economic, political, and military/strategic, further distinguishing several economic issues, notably the short term (transportation) and long-term, i.e., location, decisions. We recognize that non-economic factors may be critical in the formulation of national policies, and we have asked only whether, subject to such prior decisions which may or may not actually have the political/military effect claimed for them, these policies were then executed in the most efficient way possible. Our conclusion was that, in general, they were not: location decisions were inefficient. We also

concluded, on the other hand, that the short-term decisions -
transportation planning and operations - were essentially very efficient,
both in terms of factor inputs required for the actually achieved level
of transport output, and in terms of transport output necessary to
distribute the given amount of product.   This last result was a
conclusion that prior knowledge of Soviet writing would scarcely have
predicted, given the extensive criticism during the 1930s of transport
sector operations, both intermodal split and intramodal distribution by
the railroads. That writers spent all their criticism on transportation
rather than location, however, is itself a rebuke to the efficiency of the
economy's operation, since what it means is that industry observers,
specialists in operations, journalists, and technicians in research
institutes, were too timid to call into question the highest level
decisions of the industry, i.e., the decisions about where to place new
production capacity.

NOTES

(1) One writer, Brodskii for example, urged greater use of water routes in the third five-year plan (Brodskii, 1937). One objection peculiar to cement transport by water is that water transport would require bags or barrels to prevent hydration of the cement powder en route.

(2) One important special-purpose cement was that used for lining and sealing oil wells. Most or all of this was probably produced. at the Baku plant, near where it was consumed.

5 Efficiency in Agriculture

Besides being one of the slowest growing sectors of the national economy (see Table 2.2), Soviet agriculture has generally been believed to be extremely inefficient. The definition and analysis of efficiency, especially with a view to answering questions of systemic influences and comparative efficiency, are the subject of the present chapter.

CLASSIFICATION AND DEFINITIONS OF INEFFICIENCY

Although Soviet agriculture has generally been viewed by Western observers as being very inefficient, it is not possible to define any single summary index of inefficiency. Many of the surrogate measures which are sometimes attempted simply will not do. As evidence of inefficiency Jasny has cited the rising production costs of agricultural products in relation to key industrial products (1967, p. 212). But this shift may simply reflect the increasing attention to investment in industry and the resulting lower relative prices of industrial products, deemed necessary to industrialization, rather than agricultural inefficiencies. Rising labor input is also an inappropriate measure; if poor lands must be assimilated to raise agricultural output because of a politically prescribed goal of domestic self-sufficiency, or because of regional relocation or withdrawal of fertile lands close in, and if capital inputs are not increased disproportionately, we will find increasing labor utilization per unit output. At the same time, however, it may still be true that efficiency, defined as the best use of the resources which are applied, does actually obtain. Obviously international comparison of agricultural output per man are more questionable since they are not abstracted from differential natural resource endowments, (1) as are international comparisons relating output to total factor input (or comparisons over time), which run into numerous valuation and conceptual problems.

70

On a different plane, certain organizational and institutional features of Soviet agriculture, such as the continued existence of the private plot economy, the kolkhoz wage structure, or controversies regarding collective versus state forms of farming unit, have been taken as cause - or symptom - of inefficiency in agriculture, and ameliorative prescriptions inferred.

But even if we could imagine an aggregate measure of agricultural inefficiency, it would be of questionable value since it would provide no information on the reason for the inefficiency and, therefore, it would not assist either Soviet planners in rationalizing agriculture, or Western observers in evaluating the attempts to do so. Many such solutions are offered by Soviet and Western observers - party secretaries, government leaders, economists, academicians, and journalists - recommending or envisaging as the major remedies polities as diverse as promotion of interfarm cooperation and agro-industrial enterprises (Kosygin, 1976, p. 10), or expansion of the link (zveno) organizational structure (e.g., Smith, 1976, pp. 212-13; Nove, 1976a, p. 51). And over the past two decades policies as varied as enlargement of farm size, conversion of collective farms to state farms, discouragement of private plot agriculture, reduction of farm size, expansion of private plot agriculture, and other organizational curatives, as well as fluctuations in the rate of investment, have followed in various combinations and in hasty succession.

To see which of these policies offers most promise or, indeed, whether an altogether different approach should be followed, it is necessary to determine whether Soviet agriculture is inefficient in the first place and in what regard. It is possible that one kind of measure may be required to overcome existing inefficiency and a different action, such as greater investment in land reclamation, may be necessary to raise output further.

We begin by presenting a classificatory framework to analyze inefficiency and review the evidence bearing on the different sources of inefficiency. Four possible types of inefficiency which call for different remedies must be distinguished: 1) micro technical incompetence; 2) incentive structure inefficiency; 3) macro intrasectoral inefficiency; and 4) macro intersectoral inefficiency. These can be defined in terms of production possibility frontiers (PPF) in the following way:

1) Technical incompetence is represented by a point to the southeast of the Production Possibility Frontier in Figure 5.1. Note that Figure 5.1 represents the production possibilities for two agricultural goods denoted here as wheat and meat. It implies, therefore, that, but for technical incompetence, more of at least one agricultural product could be produced without reducing the output of other products, i.e., no additional intersectoral input reallocation is necessary to raise output. To simplify presentation we assume that, while given quantities of labor and fixed and current capital inputs could be better utilized to reach the frontier, the cost of the additional training that might be necessary to enhance the labor power as required is relatively slight. If large

investments are necessary to achieve this training, we find outselves in the situation of macro intersectoral or intrasectoral inefficiency.

2) Incentive structure inefficiency also would show up as an interior activity level in Figure 5.1. Diagrammatically, it would be indistinguishable from technical incompetence and it is very difficult to separate the two sources on the basis of available information, even though they are different conceptually. Clearly, if the incentive structure is at fault, different remedies are called for as compared with technical incompetence.

3) Macro intrasectoral inefficiency refers to outright bungling or incompetence at upper levels of administration, or even to apparently sound although incorrect distribution of investment within agriculture. It is illustrated by Figure 5.2. An additional resource input has been devoted to agriculture which could have shifted the PPF from PPF_1 to PPF_2. But because the resources were applied irrationally, the PPF shifts only to PPF_3, which is dominated by PPF_2.

4) Intersectoral inefficiency, shown in Figure 5.3, refers to irrational investment allocation between agriculture and the rest of the economy (hereinafter called industry). The PPF^1 shows the attainable output of machinery and bread. (The prime distinguishes the present discussion from the treatment of macro intrasectoral inefficiency). Starting at PPF_1', investment is distributed between agriculture and industry in a way which shifts the frontier to PPF_2'. This represents a shift in favor of industrial production. At the same time, suppose that this investment could have been distributed in such a way that PPF_3' might have been realized. As drawn, the price line V intersects PPF_3', so that intersectoral inefficiency is observed. Any combination of bread and machinery on V has a constant value. We could thus move along V to a range of output combinations which represent interior points of PPF_3'. Since PPF_3' could have been attained for the same investment or disutility as PPF_2', the cost is the same. Therefore, we could produce the output combinations on V between A and the X axis at lower cost (invest less and shift the PPF' to a point short of PPF_3'). If, on the other hand, a more agriculturally oriented investment could have shifted the frontier only as far as PPF_4', agriculture could be said to be intersectorally efficient

This classification is more detailed than the usual distinction between static and dynamic inefficiency. Our first two cases (with the simplification in the definition of technical incompetence) are both examples of static inefficiency, customarily defined conceptually as less than optimal use of existing resources, i.e., Pareto inefficiency. The second two are examples of dynamic inefficiency which might be defined as less than the maximal rate of growth attainable with an initial resource endowment. Clearly, in macro intrasectoral inefficiency a sub-maximal growth rate is achieved almost by definition (industry growth remains constant but the agricultural PPF moves less than it might with a redistribution of resources within agriculture), while under intersectoral inefficiency, the growth of one sector is promoted in excess of the preferences of society or planners, as

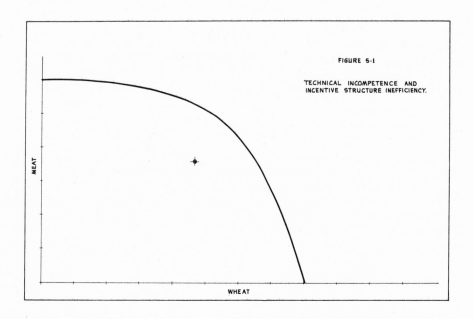

FIGURE 5-1

TECHNICAL INCOMPETENCE AND
INCENTIVE STRUCTURE INEFFICIENCY.

MEAT

WHEAT

measured by price, and at the same time encourages a growth of a different sector which is less than that preferred by planners or society. (2)

TECHNICAL INCOMPETENCE

By technical incompetence we mean bungling or lack of elementary skills or knowledge by individuals in daily farm operations. Although there are many signs of technical incompetence scattered through Jasny's writings and elsewhere, there has been little attempt to measure its total significance. Nor can large differences in output per man between the Soviet Union and Canada or the United States be taken as evidence of technical incompetence. Such highly aggregated ratios reflect the influence of numerous factors besides technical incompetence - indeed, all the other forms of inefficiency to be studied here, as well as geographical and climatic factors, which do not bear on inefficiency at all.

What is necessary for the evaluation of micro technical incompetence is to hold all other factors constant - land, climate, capital,

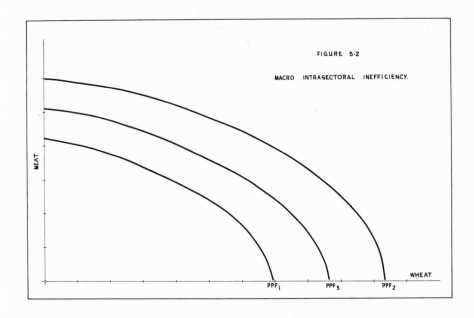

FIGURE 5-2

MACRO INTRASECTORAL INEFFICIENCY.

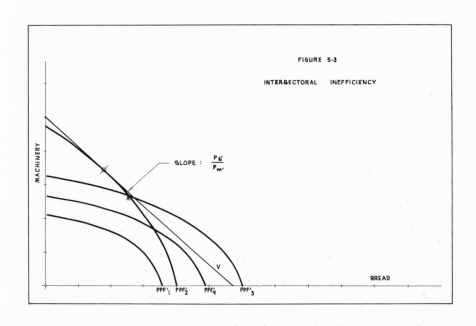

FIGURE 5-3

INTERSECTORAL INEFFICIENCY

etc., as well as incentive structure - i.e., we need something resembling a controlled experiment. There have been very few attempts to do this in either the Soviet or Western literature. Two papers that do follow such an approach are those by Alec Nove and Roy Laird (1953) and Nove (1976b), the latter a preliminary report on a larger study. While these studies do not employ the analytical framework being proposed here, and do not explicitly attempt to distinguish between technical incompetence and incentive-related inefficiency, the evidence of the first paper can be further analyzed to try to illuminate these individual sources of inefficiencies, and it is to be hoped that the large Nove study will also shed light on these factors. What then is the essence of the Nove-Laird study?

Nove and Laird conclude that kolkhoz labor utilization exceeds by 15-20 times the United States labor input on a comparable farm. In their study, soil fertility in the United States control area was thought to be similar to that on the Soviet kolkhoz in question, and some adjustments were made for qualitative differences in capital between the two countries (such as differences in tractor design) in deriving this estimate.

The excess Soviet labor input found by Nove and Laird arises for several reasons. Besides simply incompetence and lack of ability on the part of the farmers, there are effects of the incentive structure, notably the redundant weighing operations associated with the trudoden' structure. Adjusting the Nove-Laird overall data by their estimate of time spent on such activities reduces the overall labor input by 10-15%.

Other organizational-institutional features, such as the need to transport the grain to two different areas for obligatory state deliveries and for the kolkhoz store may, as the authors note, be of some importance, but it is not likely that allowing for this would make a difference of more than a few percentage points in the labor utilization ratio. (3) Accordingly, one would be left with a staggering excess labor input on the order of ten times due primarily to micro technical incompetence.

INCENTIVE STRUCTURE INEFFICIENCY

Incentive structure inefficiency shows up in several ways. First, the trudoden' system, involving inter alia piece rate premia, undoubtedly led to otherwise unnecessary labor such as weighing, sheaving, and so on. This seems to be the explanation for the excess weighing noted by Jasny (1954, p. 216) as well as that cited by Nove and Laird. A second source of low labor productivity, although it may be inefficient from a national point of view, is the attractive alternative for farm labor represented by the private plots. While the trudoden' wage system itself has frequently been held to provide inadequate incentives and to lead more directly to inefficiency, it is interesting to note in this regard that one major recent study of collective farming has concluded that this payment system probably was consistent with the goal of output maximization before it was abandoned in 1966 (Stuart, 1972, pp. 82-83).

A more general allegation concerning the inadequacy of incentives in agriculture is the separation between responsibility and earnings. Since a row is a row is a row, and the quality of care did not affect wages, it was argued, there was no financial incentive to ensure proper cultivation or to work extra hours at harvest time, administrative devices and exhortation being all that the farm manager could bring to bear. (4) Against this background, great promise attaches to the experiments with the link system as an organizational form in which members of a brigade were assigned firm responsibility and supervision over definite parcels of land. But as the best Western study of the results of the experiments showed (Pospielovsky, 1970), we do not know at what cost the fantastic results - e.g., a tripling of output per hectare, a twentyfold increase in output per man, a doubling of income per man - were achieved. Was additional capital given to the brigades to achieve these results and if so, what would this increase in capital per man have achieved with standard organization? Was labor diverted from the private plots with a consequent reduction in output there? Was there a tendency to use the most productive workers on the links? Since the sufferance of the links is very much at the whim of party bureaucrats who might have goals other than agricultural output maximazation, the release of information may be carefully keyed to the current direction of the wind. Thus, while the results seem to show strikingly the salubrious effect of catering to the self-interest of workers in agriculture, it is too early to say whether wholesale conversion would shift the agricultural sector closer to the PPF. Conceivably, if capital is diverted from other agricultural subsectors, and to the extent that the increased collective operations might come at the expense of private plot agriculture, the reported increases in output cannot be reckoned as unqualified net gains to the economy. (5)

The data in the Pospielovsky study reflect both incentive structure inefficiently directly, and incentive-related inefficiencies acting through micro incompetence. For example, we may expect that some of the problems of low labor productivity originate in misunderstanding concerning technological operations, such as failure to reckon with the uneven concentration of nutrients in chemical fertilizers and take corrective measures. (6) Introduction of the link system might provide a greater incentive to the link to disseminate knowledge among the members, reducing technical incompetence, and raising yields per man and per hectare.

MACRO INTRASECTORAL INEFFICIENCY

Macro intrasectoral inefficiency is illustrated in Figure 5.2. The production frontier existing at some point in time is given by PPF_1. A policy is adopted which could shift the frontier to PPF_2 but, as things turn out, the frontier shifts only to PPF_3. The policy decision may be a one-time investment,   or a policy which involves higher current expenditures on the wrong thing, such as injudicious selection of technology, crop policies, and land use decisions.

This is a very serious source of inefficiency in the Soviet system. Numerous examples jump to mind: Stalin's cotton expansion program in the 1930s with the tremendous opportunity costs of using the very valuable Ukrainian land for a crop to which it was ill-suited (Jasny, 1949, p. 565); Khrushchev's corn program, again with exceedingly high opportunity costs, (Jasny, 1964 and 1967); and the catalogue of technological blunders fostered by Lysenko and Viliams and amply documented by Medvedev (1969) and Joravsky (1967). Caution must be exercised here, however, to guard against criticizing every policy of staggering proportion merely because it is ambitious. The virgin lands wheat program in Kazakhstan, for example, may show low output per man or per acre but, as we noted at the start, if long-term considerations of self-sufficiency are paramount, this may be acceptable. (7)

As another example of macro intrasectoral inefficiency we might cite the Soviet neglect of the scale economies which arise in custom combining such as is practiced in North America (see Abouchar and Needles).   Reference intended here is not to the machine tractor stations, which provided a way to enforce political control over the kelkhozy and represented the physical means by which much of the grain was transferred to the state from the farms, and which were eventually disbanded for various reasons, including the growing difficulty of coordinating harvests and a policy of indenturing them through the sale of the equipment to the farms. Rather, we have in mind the custom combine operations which sweep through the major American regions, starting in Arkansas and reaching as far north as Manitoba and Saskatchewan.   There are two major Soviet belts - Moldavia, Ukraine, and European Russia comprising the first, and the Kazakh SSR, the second - in which the harvesting pattern of crops suitable for combining appears to be sufficiently spread out over time to warrant a wave of harvesting brigades, reducing the stock of machinery required for annual harvesting operations. The reduction in capital for this purpose would permit transfer of investment to other parts of the sector and an increase in labor productivity therein.

The major obstacle to the analysis of macro intrasectoral inefficiency is the lack of assessment of the programs by the Russians themselves. For understandable, even if regrettable, reasons, quantification of the cost of this inefficiency are not attempted in the USSR; even when the blunders are made by a predecessor, no great advantage from reworking the past would normally accrue to any premier or party chief, a fact to which witness is amply borne by the failure to publish Medvedev's indictment of the Lysenko tradition within the USSR.

Naturally, no agronomic or agricultural economics research institution or agency would be expected to undertake analysis of, e.g., Khrushchev's corn program while it was in progress. Thus, we not only have no studies; we have precious little data. Not enough for any definitive quantification of costs, at any rate. For all his painstaking effort in trying to determine the net result of the corn program, Jasny's analysis stops considerably short of anything like a final number for lack of a total labor input series! Medvedev's tantalizing enumeration of Lysenkoite follies cannot specify the rubles-and-kopecks cost of any particular policy. But, that final quantification cannot be made should not be interpreted to mean that the big decisions are unimportant but, rather, only that they are too big for ordinary mortals to comment on.

INTERSECTORAL INEFFICIENCY

Intersectoral inefficiency implies a distribution of resources between industry and agriculture which is inefficient in terms of the preferences of the planners themselves. That is to say, even taking as given the planners' preference for industrial development, the possibility arises that too little investment is directed into agriculture. Again, while we cannot determine how much inefficiency may arise in this source, we can at least indicate whether it has been a factor at all.

The price line V in Figure 5.3 is expressed in terms of planners' valuations. Its slope is presumed to represent the relative valuation which planners put on one unit of agricultural output relative to one unit of industrial output. Inefficiency may be said to take place if the price line intersects a production frontier which might have been realized under an investment allocation pattern other than the one actually executed.

In this kind of investigation, the deck is stacked in favor of the Soviet planners. Since the relative valuations determine the price line, and since these can never be determined objectively by an outside observer, it can always be argued that, assuming the planners to be rational, the planners' valuations will be revealed by their actions and so will always be consistent with the plan adopted. Following this line of reasoning, it would be argued that if the production possibilities frontiers are as shown in Figure 5.3, the relative valuations of bread and machinery must be less than P_b'/P_m' so that the price line tangent to PPF_2' could not intersect any point on PPF_3'. On the other hand, we do know that planners need not be rational[3] - as all the examples of macro intrasectoral inefficiency attest - so that the implied consistency need not hold.

Let us look a little more closely. It is safe to say that during the prewar period the valuation of a unit of agricultural output was extremely low relative to industrial output, so that the price line for all practical purposes approached the horizontal and no redirection of resources could have been efficient in relation to the planners' preferences. Thus, intersectoral inefficiency was probably not a characteristic of the prewar situation. We must take care not to confuse with inefficiency the generally low level of agricultural output during the 1930s, the severe shortfalls from production targets, or the dreadful havoc wreaked upon agriculture by farmers' reactions to the collectivization drives in which herd sizes fell by 50-75% from their levels before the start of the first five-year plan. It is hard to see how any alternative path to industrialization, any course of action other than collectivization even though it brought with it an immediate and tragic reaction by the peasants, could possibly have provided the food necessary to support industrialization. Certainly the experience of the 1920s when the farmers withheld the fruit of their labors against the unfavorable and deteriorating terms of trade, shown most graphically as the open blades of a pair of scissors, could hardly persuade anyone otherwise. (8)

Since World War II, the administration has set a higher valuation on agricultural output as compared with the prewar period, since by this time the country had been pointed firmly on the road to industrialization. Accordingly, the price line showing the planners' relative valuations now slopes downward. Did the postwar planners devote relatively more investment to agriculture in consonance? Although a good investment series is not available, relative growth in the agricultural and industrial capital stocks indicates that they did so. The net capital stock series of Moorsteen and Powell can be used to show this.

The net stock in agriculture (the difference between the total non-residential capital stock and the non-residential-non-agricultural capital stock) grew by amounts ranging from 29% less to 56% less than the non-residential-non-agricultural capital stock between 1928 and 1940, the variation depending on the year used as the price base. Between 1946 and 1962, the net agricultural capital stock grew faster than the industrial capital stock by amounts ranging from 22% more to 44% more, again depending on the price base. (9)

The comparison just made is a long way from refuting the existence of intrasectoral inefficiency in the postwar period, of course. Obviously, one would have to know whether the correct change in investment proportions was achieved. It merely means that we would have to look further for confirmation or refutation of the existence of intersectoral inefficiency in the postwar period although there is no overwhelming evidence of this type of inefficiency.

PROSPECTS

While it is possible that both kinds of policy may be desired, it is important to distinguish between policies designed to correct inefficiencies in the agricultural sector and those designed to promote agricultural output at the expense of industry. Only by keeping these areas distinct can we begin to assess the possible benefits of a particular policy.

From the analysis presented here, we can say that if the leadership is sincerely interested in promoting agricultural efficiency, the first requirement is to face problems honestly and not misdirect attention by grandiose and misdirected remedies such as the corn program and other policies which promote intrasectoral inefficiency, or by installing an agricultural tsar of whatever technological persuasion who seeks to impose uniform and possibly totally inappropriate solutions on a national basis.   To be sure, it is easy to give such advice and there is little certainty that it will be heeded; on the other hand, if those who do not learn from the mistakes of history are doomed to repeat them, objective bystanders can at least feel confident in predicting that mistaken absolutist policies will be no more successful in the future than they were in the past. Similarly, we can conclude that attempts to restructure agriculture - ranging from renomination of organizational forms to the institution of agro-industrial complexes and increasing specialization - will achieve little.   The first did accomplish little except reorient the typographers' jobs at <u>Statistika</u>, and the latter, for all its support by leaders as high up as Leonid Brezhnev and Alexei Kosygin, places too much reliance on scale economies and takes too little heed of soil differences and/or the benefits of crop rotation, if what is intended is complete or nearly complete specialization. (10)

This assessment assumes that the primary direction intended for the agro-industrial complex is from the farm to the large industrial processor. But as Arcadius Kahan points out (1976), this need not be the major thrust, and indeed the expression seems to mean all things to all people today, with perhaps most emphasis on the flow from industry to agriculture (for production and consumption) through greater development of small-scale industry on the farms.

According to our survey of the evidence, the major sources of inefficiency were macro intrasectoral and micro incompetence, i.e., the incentive structure and other micro systemic influences on inefficiency were less important.   Besides trying to ensure the institution of less disruptive policies at the top, as noted (i.e., reduce macro intrasectoral inefficiency), the greatest gain would then seem to lie in the direction of eliminating technical incompetence. Giving the farm workers better training should help them directly by acquiring better basic agricultural skills and by utilizing information being disseminated throughout the sector (e.g., by the experimental stations), and also by putting them in a better position to question administrative rules foisted upon them by overzealous bureaucrats. (We should note that education is not costless so that the resulting expected gains in production would not be net gains, but it is believed that the education costs are low enough in comparison to the gains, for this to be virtually an example of the first type of inefficiency.)

How bad is the rural education picture today? Very bad. This is clear from statistics on education levels in David Carey's 1973 study. Thus, as of 1970 (p. 623) fully half of the rural workers had only 0-3 years of primary education.   Adding in the 3 out of 10 workers with incomplete secondary education (i.e., grades 4-8), makes a total of 80% of rural workers with what may be regarded as less than minimal educational qualifications. Since the rural worker group presumably includes some non-farm workers (village artisans and shopkeepers) who may be presumed to have more education, the percentage of farm workers with these low qualifications is probably larger. By contrast, the urban worker group had relatively only half as many in the 0-3 year group and only 57% in all in the 0-8 year group. To be sure, the picture for the rural workers has improved in the last 20 years (in 1959 the proportion with subminimal qualifications was 90%), but the improvement among urban workers has been even greater, the share in the low educational attainment group (less than grade 8) falling from 74% to 57% over the period.

Regarding training of specialists, less than 14% (Carey, p. 602) of all enrollments in specialized secondary schools are in agricultural programs while in higher educational institutions, the share is around 7.5%. (11)

Interestingly, the 1976-1980 "Basic Directions" stress the need for better varieties, cropping methods, etc., and the development of experimental production centers ("Basic Directions", p. 14), but say nothing about education. If educational levels have been inadequate in the past, they will be even more so in future if there is any serious attempt to develop such methods and mechanisms, to help to put "science and leading practice into life."

A SYSTEMIC COMPARISON

We have seen that the Soviet economy has historically been characterized by four kinds of agricultural inefficiency and that there is a strong presumption that at least the first three of these inefficiencies have continued to the present. We now turn to the questions whether these sources of inefficiency are inherent in a socialist economy, whether they are in any way restricted to such an economy or are merely like to be more serious there. Table 5.1 shows the probable occurrence of the several types of inefficiency in five different economic systems: 1) the actual Soviet system, 2) the theoretical socialist system, 3) the underdeveloped market economy, 4) the North American capitalist economy, and 5) the idealized perfectly competitive economy.

According to the table, there is no inefficiency in the perfectly competitive system. The usual assumptions of perfect competition - rationality, perfect information, and utility maximization - combine to preclude inefficiency in that system. This contrasts with the theoretical socialist model based on Marxian principles, as traditionally conceived in the West, under which the failure to reflect the differential advantages of variously situated lands could lead to inefficient land allocation between agriculture and the rest of the economy, as well as within agriculture, thus giving rise to both inter- and intrasectoral macro inefficiencies. (The constraints of the Marxian legacy on the price system will be analyzed in detail in Chapter 7.) Of course, we could not tell how large such inefficiencies would be in the theoretical socialist model, but I would speculate that they would not be terribly significant.

We turn next to the real economies. All three are characterized by incentive structure inefficiency. The Soviet case was described above.

TABLE 5.1. Possible Areas of Inefficiency in Agriculture in Five Economic Systems

Type of Inefficiency	Actual Soviet Economy	Theo-retical Socialist Economy	Under-developed Market Economy	North American Economy	Perfect-ly Com-petitive Model
1. Technical incompetence	yes	no	yes	yes	no
2. Incentive structure inefficiency	yes	no	yes	yes	no
3. Macro intra-sectoral ineffiency	yes	yes	yes	no	no
4. Inter-sectoral Inefficiency	prewar: no postwar: ?	yes	yes	yes	no

Wherein do we find incentive structure inefficiency in the underde-veloped economy and the North American economy?

The North American problem - which is probably more important in the United States than in Canada, and which has probably been more important in the past than today - relates to farmers' responses to the price incentives facing them. We are thinking here primarily of such programs as land withdrawals in response to government payments. While these actions are, of course, efficient from the farmer's viewpoint, they are inefficient from the viewpoint of output maximi-zation over time, which is the criterion of efficiency that we have in mind. Other less direct stimuli to inefficiency involve subsidized rail and/or road pricing which encourages farmers to remain on submarginal land or to grow the wrong crops. A good example of this is the recent recommendation by a Canadian federal inquiry commission to rebuild some prairie trackage and continue giving explicit subsidies to certain grain producers, not to speak of maintaining the historical legislated rail rates for prairie grain movement, in defiance of naive assumptions of what would constitute a proper environment for the efficient operation of the invisible hand. (12)

Turning now to the developing economy, we see that inefficiencies occur in three of the four rows. Technical incompetence is of the same type as that in the Soviet economy, and is probably influenced by the same forces - lack of knowledge of production methods brought about by poor dissemination of information and low educational levels.

Incentive structure inefficiency shows up directly in the reluctance to undertake improvements on land worked but not owned, and it also shows up indirectly in intrasectoral inefficiency. To take Brazil in the 1960s, for example, we find a traditional preference for growing coffee over beans, although the country was starving for beans while coffee clogged the warehouses, even to the extent that the income which the coffee ultimately brought was frequently less than spent to replace worn out sacks. The reasons were twofold: 1) the traditional social prestige attaching to coffee growing as opposed to bean production, together with 2) the government support prices for coffee, in turn the result of political pressure by growers. This mechanism can also be the stimulus to intersectoral efficiency.

This analysis has shown that all of the real world economies contain some inefficiency in agriculture, as does the theoretical socialist model. The theoretical capialist model, with its highly unrealistic assumptions, is alone in having none.

NOTES

(1) The 1973 study by Douglas Whitehouse and Joseph Havelka is a careful attempt at international comparisons. Trying especially to evaluate output on a consistent basis, they show that output per man in the United States is eleven times as high as in the Soviet Union. As they also show, United States manpower is armed with twenty times as many trucks (p. 354). But even if one could make an adjustment for the capital difference, what of land quality, climate, etc. Now, while the authors of such studies do not usually explicitly draw conclusions about superiority of one or the other economy, many readers do draw such conclusions.

(2) The notions being exploited here are also not the same as productivity measurements over time (either macro or sectoral) which do not really get at the issue of whether the economy is producing as much as it could be. This distinction was nicely stressed by Judith Thornton in an early discussion of the measurement of inefficiency (1964, p. 516).

(3) Other sources of high labor input on kolkhoz that might be confounded with sheer micro incompetence in summary calculations of farm labor productivity - although it was not in this study which related to field workers exclusively - would include clerical labor necessary to calculate trudodni.

(4) And administrative levers can be notoriously ineffective. While evidence relating to the cost of these levers is extremely informal, D. Gale Johnson has recently provided evidence which can help to evaluate the cost of one administrative lever, the regulation concerning herd numbers. Because the marginal meat/feed ratio increases with increasing size (over the relevant range), it would be more efficient to feed a given amount to a smaller herd and produce larger animals. But owing to an administrative herd size rule, farmers were kept from doing this, with an excess input estimated around 25% (Johnson, 1974, p. 55).

(5) Actually, the assignment of land parcels to individual squads or brigades has been attempted sporadically since the 1930s. Jasny reports on some of the advantages and disadvantages of these methods in his magnum opus (1949, pp. 334-337).

(6) That variation of nutrients in Soviet chemical fertilizers is a serious problem that has been pointed out many times by Western and Soviet writers. See for example, Conklin, 1969, p. 160.

(7) As a general remark, one might argue that economists might do well to be a little more willing to accept as economically justified over the long term policies which appear to be purely political in nature in the short run.

(8) The best intellectual history of the period is Alexander Erlich's book, with Dobb and Jasny (1949) supplying the details of the developments taking place.

(9) Calculated from Tables T-16 to T-21 of Richard Moorsteen and Raymond Powell (1966). No Soviet series on net investment in agriculture has been published (Schinke, 1972, p. 256).

(10) A recent study in Lithuania describing several crop optimizing programming models leads to an increase in grain from its present share up to a maximum of only 36% of total cropped area, with flax, grasses, and intertilled crops accounting for the rest. Net income under programming variants rise by as much as 18-24%. Even allowing for some scale economies in the agro-industrial complex, it seems unlikely that they would be great enough to overcome the implied loss in net income, which here can be taken as social product, that would follow from devoting all land on this farm to grain (Grude, 1975).

(11) The share for agricultural specialists in higher educational institutions is estimated by adding to Carey's share of total enrollments in non-engineering agricultural specialities, the 7.5% figure is the share of engineering graduates in 1970 who had agricultural specialities (Bronson, 1973, p. 588).

(12) For an analysis of these recommendations see Abouchar, 1977.

6 Efficiency in Industry

More than agriculture, Soviet industry has often been said to be extremely inefficient and, given its role as the leading sector of the economy, this inefficiency has been viewed as a much greater source of weakness. Western study of the efficiency of Soviet industry has been approached in many ways. All are useful in gaining insights into the degree of efficiency in industry, but some are capable of giving us greater direction and information than others, none being exhaustive by itself. We distinguish the following four approaches:

Behavioral analysis, providing empirical-institutional information on Soviet managerial behavior;

Macro productivity measurement;

Empirical industry analysis; and

Price-theoretic analysis.

Price-theoretic analysis, which has often been used to reach general conclusions on Soviet economic efficiency, will be deferred to Chapter 7 for extended discussion. In the present chapter we will treat the first three approaches to the study of industrial efficiency, these, especially the first two, being approaches most often pursued.

BEHAVIORAL ANALYSIS OF INDUSTRIAL MANAGERS

This approach seeks to analyze the implications for Soviet industrial performance which follow from expectations concerning Soviet managerial behavior. Such studies usually conclude that Soviet industry is inefficient because managerial self-interest conflicts with the planner's will. This view neglects the existence of internal checks and balances

86

which, at the least, reduce the severity of managerial response to the given stimuli. We will consider here the most important of the stimuli which are supposed to induce undesirable behavior, the checks and balances that may exist and the probable effect on industry performance. We consider the seven most widely cited problems.

Plan bargaining

The major indicator of enterprise performance is gross output, either expressed in physical terms such as tons of pig iron, or in synthetic physical units or, when output mix is very diverse, in money terms. Managers are paid a premium over their basic salary for monthly performance and this is seen by some observers as a source of weakness. The premium depends upon the category of the manager, and on the industry. Rather large premia are awarded for exact plan fulfilment, ranging up to 100% premium payments in the coal industry, and different scales are applied to each percentage point of overfulfilment (Berliner, 1957, p. 30). This naturally leads managers to hide production possibilities to try to get a low plan and then overfulfil it, instead of working at high pressure on a continuing basis. However, the administrators at a higher level must soon become aware of this possibility: assigning targets partakes of the nature of bargaining between opposing parties, each interested in certain aspects of the production schedule. But in the absence of this bonus arrangement, managers would still want to receive plans which they could fulfil as easily as possible. That is, normal considerations of personal interest would lead to a system of tension between plan formulators and plan executants in any event, since a manager who regularly just fulfilled his targets would be given higher targets.

Falsification of reports

Since the manager receives a large bonus for exact plan fulfilment, and high premia for each percentage overfulfilment, there is thought to be an incentive to falsify reports. This may consist either of outright falsification or "borrowing," which means that performance is overreported one month, with the overstatement being repaid the next. But the nature of the premium system itself prevents this to some extent. If he overfulfilled by 1% this month, a manager would receive both his premium for exact fulfilment, which is usually 5-8 times as high as the premium for overfulfilment, as well as the latter premium. But then if he "repaid" next month not only would he forego his overfulfilment premium, but he would also lose the fulfilment premium. Thus, he would be considerably worse off than if he had just fulfilled in both periods. Thus, there is a limit to the amount of "borrowing" for rational managers.

In any event, one has to ask whether any really serious harm is done by borrowing in the first place. The harm done is mainly to the planning procedures of the supervisory organs, since planners might believe they have greater stocks than is in fact the case. But since it is unlikely that this either continues for very long or that these "advances" become very large, it probably does very little harm.

Distortions in output mix

The objection here is that the manager systematically produces the wrong things. The classic Pravda cartoon showing a plant manager standing by his plan's monthly output of nails - a single nail suspended by a crane - ridicules the tendency to be guided by the nature of the target: when nail targets are given in weight, economies of scale dictate the production of spikes; when outputs are decreed in units, tacks are produced. While this is almost sure to be the case to some extent, it is all too easy to exaggerate the severity of the problem. For example, the scale economies in shoe production would not be so great as to justify exclusive concentration on only three or four styles or sizes. To what extent does the information in the Soviet press represent a general phenomenon? And to what extent is this scene repeated continually in the press as a warning for managers to walk the straight and narrow path? It is impossible to assess, but it seems likely that a good deal of it is strictly for instructional and admonitory purposes.

Other aspects of output mix distortion come readily to mind. It is often complained that managers concentrate on a materials-intensive product mix. Since labor is usually scarce, managers can produce greater money value of output by using expensive materials, e.g., producing fur hats rather than felt hats with the same labor input. But that it is possible to produce fur hats means that there is some demand for this commodity and that the planners do want some fur hats. Why should we automatically conclude that there must be objections to the production of this product? Obviously, it depends upon how many fur and how many felt hats are produced. But on the basis of the traditional arguments alone, there is no certainty that an undesirable mix will be produced.

Spare parts production is frequently thought to be a problem. This may well be, but it does not necessarily follow from logical considerations alone. Indeed, one could imagine a plethora of spares; since in constructing any sophisticated machine some parts might be missing, it might be cheaper to send out the machine as a bunch of parts rather than hold up final assembly and await the necessary missing links. To be sure, there may be lack of communication between the part users and the producers, but this need not depend upon the incentive structure.

Too much local investment

It is often complained that the nature of the incentive system, together with supply unreliability, influences managers to ensure themselves a supply of critical materials by producing too many things locally. This leads to too much local investment undertaken for this purpose. On the other hand, the manager is often faulted for reluctance to innovate.

Reluctance to innovate

The manager trying to play it safe will be reluctant to innovate, since innovation may lead to underfulfilment of the targets that are assigned. If he innovated more there would be serious difficulties in assimilating new production, which would tell on the manager's performance. This diagnosis conflicts with the observation that managers make too many attempts to revise their output mix in order to secure higher prices for their products, which would naturally affect their gross output measured in ruble terms. How can this contradiction be reconciled? To some extent, it cannot and need not - forces will be at work pushing the manager in different directions. Just as in the West, a manager would want to produce high quality products in order to see them, but not products which are higher quality than the money he can get for them, which depends upon the demand characteristics of the market. In the USSR we must also expect that there will be different influences at work. While these forces were unharnessed for most of the Soviet period, merely existing and working in opposing directions, some attempt has been made recently to formalize them by relating new product prices to the period of assimilation (Berliner, 1975; Grossman, 1977).

Storming

It is often observed that the tempo of activity steps up towards the end of the month as the plant hurries to fulfil its monthly quota. As a result, output is somewhat uneven during the month, falling down in the first week and rising during the last. Some unevenness in production is certainly to be expected, but it can scarcely be construed to constitute a greater transgression. This frequently takes place in the West where the satisfaction of getting out "one more order this month" causes an increase in work tempo towards the end of the month. The alternative to higher paced production towards the end of the month might be average, but generally lower production throughout the month. If this is the case, storming does make a positive contribution.

The "tolkach" or pusher

The tolkach is frequently inveighed against in the Soviet press, and it is easy to interpret this rebuke as a proscription of the activities of the pusher, who serves to smooth the way between supplies and users. The pusher, either on the payroll of an enterprise or sometimes working on his own, does build up an extensive knowledge of the availability and sources of supply, and he puts this knowledge to use, for a fee, advising users where to find scarce products. It is to be expected, also, that fees paid for this service are actually dispensed as bribes to suppliers to direct outputs to favored firms.

But we should be careful not to confuse rebuke, which may merely represent the official attempt to maintain respectability and set an example for society, and anathema. Soviet officials are aware of the positive good done by pushers and, indeed, it is likely that on the whole they do make a positive contribution. They accumulate vast stores of information, which would otherwise have to be accumulated at some cost. By finding goods which were otherwise overlooked, they speed up circulation, reducing the time of immobilization of the factor inputs which these products represent. And to the extent that they bias delivery in favor of the enterprises best able to pay they are probably doing a worthwhile service, since it is probably enterprises which do have the means to pay that are in the highest priority lines of production anyway.

Many variations could be given on these motifs but enough has been said by now to show the difficulty inherent in the attempt to assess this kind of information and evaluate the overall impact of such occurrences. It is by no means certain that people will respond as believed, or that the behavior is general, or that, even if it is, the consequences are so harmful, even if they do conflict with certain administratives rules.

The truth is that, while not all managers behave correctly all of the time, it is far from being the case that they are all for behaving perversely all of the time. There are many reasons to believe that they will not always behave as naive expectations might suggest. For example, borrowing has limits due to other influences which must be taken into account. To be specific, borrowing when it does happen is almost certainly not so disruptive anyway. Similarly, the other consequences: producing an output mix which maximizes gross output by using the most abundant material, whether labor, some particular raw material, energy, etc., is quite rational and would be applauded in a market economy. When we criticize it in the Soviet economy, we are inherently assuming that the mix that is produced is at variance with the plan for that enterprises. Now, it may be at variance with the plan, but possibly this means that the plan was a bad one and, while it may offend the egos of officials, it may be better for the economy for a plant to produce from the resources which it does have at its disposal. Accordingly, this sort of behavior should often be applauded.

We should not be surprised that when we take account of other stimuli the results will not be as predicted by a naive model. To help appreciate this point of view, suppose we turn the picture around and try to imagine a visiting Soviet observer trying to make judgments about the West if he gives his imagination free rein on the basis of a model which fails to take account of all the influences at work. For example, on finding that local ski conditions are reported by the resort operator rather than by an impartial consumers' interest agency, our visitor might conclude that ski conditions will be reported as excellent everywhere between December 15 and April 15. But adjusting such a view by the recognition that the ski operator would very quickly lose his credibility if he did this, the visitor would conclude that this is not the case, although still allowing that there may be some tendency to exaggerate. But again the visitor would have to recognize that, within a season or less, skiers would catch on to this reporting of skiing conditions and would know how to interpret the reports; the veteran would have learned it once and would continue thereafter to make the necessary adjustments. Such a view could be further elaborated upon to allow for an occasional operator who decided to lie only to the newcomers (if he could separate them out) and mulct them during the first few months of their introduction to the sport, losing them as customers thereafter.

Similarly, our imaginary visitor might conclude that a university professor, since he will be given copies of books which he assigns to class upon request, might change his textbook whenever he wanted to increase his library holdings. But real costs would be imposed upon him by getting these free textbooks since he would have to revise his notes accordingly. Thus once again, when we take account of additional factors, our original naive expectation breaks down.

MACRO PRODUCTIVITY MEASUREMENT

What we really want to know when we ask about the economic efficiency of industry is whether the industrial sector is operating on a production frontier. Production frontiers have been illustrated a number of times already. In a two- or even three-commodity economy we may be able to draw the frontier, but in a real economy with thousands of commodities it is impossible to do so, because of both physical constraints imposed by the limitations of three-dimensional space and the lack of data. Guided by such an objective, however, many researchers have tried a different approach, the measurement of total factor productivity. In essence, this approach shows the relationship between actually observed output and the level of output which is warranted by specified input levels. This approach has been applied to the study of a number of economies and time periods, having been pioneered in the study of the United States economy.

This indirect approach would seem unexceptionable, appearing to have a traditional microeconomic counterpart in the private firm, for which net profit (net factor productivity) is investigated and acted upon by the market every month or quarter by comparing total revenue (actually observed gross output) with total input or cost (warranted output). But whereas analysis of the private firm can or, at least does, start from the assumption of input cost minimization to attain the actual physical production levels, there is no equally appealing method of determining warranted output at the macroeconomic level. Two problems are involved: 1) determining what factor inputs actually were combined in the production of the observed output, and 2) deciding what output these input levels actually would warrant (what production function to use).

To answer the second question first, several different types of function, each exhibiting different characteristics believed to be reasonable and to reflect the underlying laws of production, have been proposed. Since the reservations presented below apply to all of the specifications of functional form, we will restrict our attention to the one which has been the most generally advocated for Western analysis and also the one most used for the Soviet economy. This is the Cobb-Douglas production function, a two-factor function which hypothesizes a multiplicative relationship between labor and capital inputs, in which the marginal product of each factor is decreasing when the other is held constant, while proportional increases in both together result in an increase in the same proportion. This function has the form $Y(t) = AL(t) K(t)^{(1-\alpha)}$ where $Y(t)$ is warranted industrial output in year t, $L(t)$ and $K(t)$ are labor and capital inputs in year t, and α and $(1-\alpha)$ are the marginal products of labor and capital respectively. This warranted output is compared to output of a base year, and then this growth in warranted output is compared with the growth of actual output. The difference is usually termed the net total factor productivity, measuring as it is thought to do the total increase beyond that which can be imputed to the input factors. This is the essential procedure developed, with various and applied modifications, over a wide range of economics and time periods.

The major inconsistency with efficiency measurement which is implicit in this approach stems from the way the marginal productivities are conceived and measured. For α we usually take the share of wage income in total income, the justification for this procedure being that in equilibrium the wage is equal to the marginal product of labor. However, if we assume such an equilibrium for every year of the series, and use for each year the share of wage income for that year, if the net productivity is calculated to be positive, it is really inefficiency rather than efficiency which is implied, since it means that prices in industry are not adjusting to equate wages and capital returns to the marginal products of labor and capital. If on the other hand, net productivity of factors is calculated to be zero, this aspect at least of efficiency - prices reflecting true scarcities - is being attained!

What is frequently done in fact is to use as the marginal productivity coefficients the relationships existing in some base year. In this case it is not clear what is being measured. The procedures applied to the Soviet Union - which share whatever limitations in interpretation the same procedures applied to Western economies suffer from - do show a respectable measured productivity, though, around 2-3% (Thornton, 1970; Noren, 1966), which compares not at all unfavorably with estimates for Western countries.

This basic contradiction remains troublesome and has not been adequately answered in the literature on productivity studies. The studies then can be justified only if we first acknowledge that we would not expect instantaneous, frictionless shifts in prices to accommodate changes in the scarcities in any economy, that is, that the price mechanism was indeed inefficient.

EMPIRICAL ANALYSIS OF INDIVIDUAL INDUSTRIES

As we have seen, the two traditional approaches to the analysis of industrial efficiency - econometric measurement of factor productivity and behavioral analysis of industrial managers - both have shortcomings. The factor productivity approach depends critically on the shape chosen for the production function, the pricing of factor inputs, qualitative and quantitative adjustments for labor, the measurement of output itself, and so on. Conceptual dilemmas lurk behind such apparently innocuous decisions as the choice of fixed versus variable weights and, if fixed, the year whose factor shares should be used.

The behavioral approach - studying the probable implications for national economic performance of Soviet managerial behavior - generally concludes that Soviet industry is inefficient because managerial self-interest will conflict with the planner's will. But, we have seen, many of the inferences based on anecdotal evidence neglect the existence of internal checks and balances which vitiate much or most of the hypothesized perverse managerial response to the given stimuli, just as a Soviet observer might make serious errors about Western behavior if he allowed himself to see only part of the scene. As a result, most studies of managerial behavior leave the reader with the impression that Soviet industry must be very inefficient indeed.

A third possibility is to study operations and organization of individual industries. This approach requires great care whether in the West or the East. The first question is what aspects or indicators can best shed light on efficiency. In a competitive economy, the existence of zero profits (allowing proper return for managers) is supposed to indicate efficient operation. Since we frequently have regulated monopoly industries with rates keyed to a cost base, there is no compulsion for the firm to minimize cost for a given output, i.e., to behave efficiently, so that we may have zero profit coexisting with inefficiency. Other problems include the possibility of hiding excess profits in the form of managerial salaries. Moreover, if the input prices for the industry do not represent social costs, as they frequently do not (e.g., they do not usually reflect the cost of pollution or pollution abatement, or the provision of highway services and other transportation infrastructure, etc.), even an industry which appears to be competitive might show a zero profit picture but involve inefficiency from the social point of view. We must recognize the existence of such limitations in the West.

Although it is impossible to reach definitive answers about efficiency in an industry on the basis of summary indicators, we can look at certain aspects of the operation of an industry to get an idea of whether it is operating efficiently or not, the main aspects being those bearing on the technological adaptation in the industry. Unfortunately, very few Soviet industries have been studied from this point of view. Part of the reason is that most industries are extremely complex, and looking at various indicators gives ambiguous results. For example, should an industry's performance be adjudged superior if it introduces products which make extensive use of vinyl components? Does the use of more alloys indicate superior performance? The answer, of course, is that such unequivocal statements are seldom or never justified. Technological rollover can never be taken as an end in itself.

One industry which is somewhat easier to evaluate from the

viewpoint of its various technological indicators, however, is the hydraulic cement industry which is marked by a number of critical and relatively unambiguous indicators of performance. A survey of this industry during the postwar period suggests that it has been efficient in its technological evolution and in its performance generally, with one or two notable exceptions that would seem relatively easy to correct. We start the analysis with a short survey of the industry and its postwar growth. We then present the evidence on the important efficiency-related aspects of industry performance (location and transport utilization, production technology including productivity, and standards).

SUMMARY OF POSTWAR DEVELOPMENT
OF THE CEMENT INDUSTRY

Between 1940 and 1976 cement production grew at 8.9% a year, one of the highest growth rates in Soviet heavy industry, exceeding steel production (5.9%), petroleum extraction (8.1%), but lagging slightly behind electric power production (9.1%) and further behind the growth of the chemical industry, expressed in rubles (11.3%). In terms of annual tonnage, its 1976 output of 124 million tons exceeded pig iron production (105.4 million tons) by nearly 20%, although it fell 20 million tons short of steel output. (1)

Annual output of hydraulic cements by major type is shown in Table 6.1. (2) Unfortunately, nowhere is a consistent table published showing the breakdown by type over the entire period, and we have had to dovetail series from several sources and rely on scattered information on product mix to produce this table. Especially notable is the absence of any consistent and careful breakdown since 1962, the year the cement handbook (Spravochnik po proizvodstvu tsementa) was published, and the data that appears in the press since then is very scanty and contains errors (see note to Table 6.1).

Notwithstanding the materials intensiveness of cement production - 1.5 tons of calcium carbonate, .4 ton of clay, and .3 ton of coal (when used as the basic fuel) per ton of portland cement - rational cement industry location tends to be market-oriented for two reasons: 1) input materials are widely found, and 2) scale economies in production are small relative to transport costs. Market orientation of production has been further encouraged by the development of gas technology, since gas can usually be delivered at costs which are competitive with coal even in the mining regions.

Cement technology in the postwar period has developed in the direction of larger kilns and automation of the more readily mechanizable operations. These and other technological developments are not important enough to exert a strong pull on location, however, since the lower production costs of the larger plant scale, and the greater concentration they imply, cannot offset the higher transport costs that concentration of production entails.

The industry continues to be vertically and horizontally unintegrated. While slag wastes from steel production and a limited number of other complementarities exist (Grokhotov and Kropotov, pp. 3-5),

TABLE 6.1.   Annual Hydraulic Cement Output, by Major Types, 1913-1970, Selected Years (millions of tons)

Year	Total	Portland	Portland-Pozzolan	Portland-Slag	Others	Portland as Percent of Total
1913	1.8					
1928	1.8					
1936	5.9	4.4	.6	.9	-	74.1
1937	5.4					
1940	5.7	3.6	.3	1.2	.5	64.0
1950	10.2	5.2	1.2	3.3	.5	50.2
1955	22.5	10.0	3.0	7.8	1.6	44.6
1958	36.7	16.4	6.1	13.4	.8	44.7
1961	50.0	23.4	7.7	18.7	0.2	46.8
1962	56.3	29.6	7.5	19.1	0.1	52.6
1964 (a)	64.9	45.4	2.9	14.9	1.6	70.0
1966 (a)	80.0					
1968	87.5	55.6	6.0	24.2	1.7	63.5
1972	104.29	67.0				64.2
1974	115.1	74.9				65.1
1976	124.2	80.6				64.8
1977	130.8 (plan)					

(a)   Partially estimated

Sources: 1913-1968, Abouchar, 1976; 1972-1977, Narkhoz, various years.

nearly all hydraulic cement is still produced by cement plants. Some imagination has been shown in raw materials diversification.   One example is the Leningrad region, traditionally short of fuel and calcium carbonates, where gas-shale has been made to substitute simultaneously for fuel and some of the clay and lime raw materials, as well as in joint production of, e.g., iron alloys and aluminous cement at a cement-metallurgical plant in the 1950s (Loginov, 1959, pp. 216-217). This is still extremely insignificant, and also quite understandable in view of the ubiquity of conventional raw materials, and the widespread availability of slag and pozzolan constituents which have come to be very extensively used since the mid-1930s.

Likewise, there has been virtually no move towards integration with final production processes. Precast concrete components and, to a lesser extent, asbestos cement products offer the most obvious possibilities for vertical integration, although concrete component integration is not likely to foster any great economies, while failure to develop integration based on asbestos cement products may simply reflect the greater advantages of other building materials and inconsequential use of cement for this purpose (perhaps .5-.7 million tons in the mid-70s. (3) We have, then, an industry with relatively simple output mix and production technology. This makes analysis much easier than analysis of efficiency in the production of machinery, consumers durables, clothing, or construction.

The average length of haul of cement was shown in Table 4.1 of Chapter 4. After the very long hauls of the 30s, which exceeded the pre-World War I haul by as much as 300%, the average haul has fallen to levels a little higher than those of the Tsarist period. Since cement consumption continues to be very dispersed nationally, and since the high pre-war average haul was due, as we saw in Chapter 4, not to irrational shipping operations but rather to an unsatisfactory location pattern, it is to a radical regional realignment that we must look as the source of the postwar reduction in transport input. The details of the postwar realignment of production and consumption are given in Abouchar (1976). The essence of the regional realignment was a move towards self-sufficiency. This tendency, in Eastern Siberia and the Far East was especially marked and had especially favorable results on transport costs, since theirs was the most transport-intensive cement consumption. Thus, between 1940 and 1970, the relative deficit fell from 100% to 5% and from 52% to 18% in these two regions, respectively. Since the average hauls to these regions from the traditional supply areas (Ukraine, the lower Volga, or southwest Russia) ranged from 6,000 kilometers (Eastern Siberia) to 10,000 kilometers (Far East), this increased self-sufficiency was bound to have a remarkably salubrious effect on the national average length of haul. Against this reduction of 50-70% we must compare the production cost increase implicit in the shift. Since 1) in the prewar period total national cement transport costs were approximately equal to production costs; 2) eastern production costs are roughly twice as high as costs in the west; and 3) the eastern regions account for about 1/7 of total consumption, the net reduction in average total delivered real cost implied by the postwar, as compared with the prewar, location pattern to service the postwar consumption pattern is around 20-25%.

Production Technology

Scale

The size of the kiln and number of kiln lines are the main sources of scale economies. Estimates of cost reduction in moving from the largest prewar kiln (108 meters) to kilns up to 185 meters in length are not available, but scattered data on reduction of fuel or labor inputs testify to the advantages of larger kilns. Kiln size distribution for 1964 is shown in Table 6.2.

TABLE 6.2. Kiln Size and Relative Capacity, 1964

Length of kiln (meters)	Percent of total clinker capacity
185	1.5
170	16.8
150	31.8
135	3.3
127-9	9.8
118	4.6
All others	32.2
Total	100.0

Source: Astanskii and Liusov, p. 1.

If too little is known about kiln scale economies, the plant size cost function is probably more difficult to evaluate. Loginov has argued that plant size economies are appreciable - capital costs falling by 70% between 60,000 ton and 90,000 ton capacity, with average total production cost declining by about 2/3, and a reduction of over 40% in many cases when annual capacity rises from 450,000 to 900,000 tons (Loginov, 1955, pp. 3-4). In a severe criticism of these results, G.G. Belov has argued that these estimates were based on empirical observations relating to widely different equipment age and regional cost structures, and that in fact the technological scale economies are much smaller, their measurement being very sensitive to shipping distances for fuels and additives. Belov estimated a unit cost reduction of about 11% as plant size doubles to 900,000 tons a year (1955, p. 21).

Plant scale has increased continually and substantially since the war. For example, while the prewar industry had 2/3 of its output in plants smaller than 200,000 tons, less than one per cent of 1968 capacity was in such small plants. Moreover, as the comparison between 1958 and

1968 in Table 6.3 shows, the trend towards larger scale has persisted even in the last fifteen years. This is not intended as criticism of the prewar industry - far from it, indeed, since in the prewar industry few regions had a market for more than 200,000 tons a year, so that small scale was proper. In fact, the smaller scale of the prewar industry represented a rationalist victory over the gigantomania of some Soviet planners who held sway during the first five-year plan. But the large scale of the postwar industry was accompanied by the sharp declines in average haul, noted earlier, and, indeed, even the trend towards concentration in 1958-68 was accompanied by a reduction of around 10% in average haul. Could a further economically significant reduction have been achieved during this decade by a reduced emphasis on large scale? This is a tempting hypothesis, given the 135% rise in annual output (Table 6.1). But if we made the reasonable assumption that most of this growth was consumed in proportion to the 1958 regional consumption pattern, we must conclude that there were no major new markets that would have consumed a large share of the production increase. In this case, it is unlikely that the transport cost reductions in the by-then traditional market areas would have justified the higher cost of smaller plants. If a conservative estimate of the long-run cost function, such as Belov's, is accepted, retention of the smaller scale pattern of the mid-50s would have raised average real production costs by around 15%. Assuming that real transport costs at the time were 50% as high as production costs, a 30% decline in transport would have been required just to offset the higher costs of the smaller scale production. In other words, the average haul in 1968 would have had to be around 320 kilometers just to break even if smaller production scale had been chosen.

TABLE 6.3. Industry Plant Size Distribution, 1958 and 1968.

Size of plant (000 tons annual capacity)	1958 Share of total production accounted for by this size plant	1968 Share of total capacity accounted for by this size plant
less than 200	26.0	0.8
201 - 500	23.4	3.8
501 - 1,000	14.3	29.7
1,001 - 1,500	20.8	22.6
1,501 - 2,000	9.1	18.4
greater than 2,000	6.5	24.7
Total	100.0	100.0
In plants larger than 1,000,000 tons	36.4	65.7

Sources: 1958, Spravechnik, p. 837; 1968, Liusev, 1970, p. 9.

Fuel

Since World War II gas has come to play the main role in the cement industry's fuel balance, accounting for nearly 50% of the caloric capacity of the industry's fuel consumption in 1962, coal (39.3%), oil (11.1%), and other fuels (2.1%) comprising the rest (Spravochnik, p. 843). Gas utilization has continued to grow, its total consumption nearly tripling between 1960 and 1966, according to Robert Campbell (p. 214), while cement output grew by 2/3, suggesting that most of the new capacity was fired by gas.

It is undoubtedly extremely rational to use gas in the cement industry. First, as Campbell shows, even though gas transmission costs (operating costs and capital costs, including 10% interest) are higher than all other forms of energy except low-grade coal and electric power, the delivered costs of gas in all major regions are much lower than those of other fuels. This is due to its very low production costs, which are about 16% of the cost of oil and 4% of the cost of coal extraction (Campbell, pp. 209, 211).

In the second place, capital and operating cost of cement plants are also lower when gas is used, since storage and coal-grinding are avoided with their attendant investment, electric power, and labor requirements (Gudkov et al., pp. 3-4). Life of kiln linings is extended, with reduced frequency of kiln shutdown; the Novorossiissk "Proletarii" plant reported increases of up to 100% in lining life and an average increase of 45% (Zakharova, p. 7). This was exceptional, undoubtedly, and while data are not available on a systematic basis, gas use is an important factor in raising national average kiln operating rates from 75% in 1950 to 87% in 1969 (Narkhoz, 69, p. 242). This was taking place even under the introduction of new long kilns which, as we have seen, generally had a difficult break-in period. Gas also permits more even heat control and more uniform clinker and gives a better product.

The only drawback of gas is the greater fuel-dust loss which accompanies it. No quantitative information has been published on this, however, and it can be partly overcome by adjusting the heat exchange devices (Zakharova, p. 6).

The low production and transportation cost of gas together with reduced costs when working with gas, make it very attractive, and its increasing use reflects a rational technological policy. Perhaps the clearest testimony to the dominance of gas is the change in the treatment of fuel between the 1959 and 1963 editions of Lur'e's standard treatise on portland cement; the 1959 edition shows some hypothetical cost relationships for a standard operating regime consisting of limestone, clay, and coal (pp. 344-345) while the standard regime for the calculations in the 1963 edition consists of limestone, clay, and gas (pp. 390-392).

Electric power

Most cement plant operations use electricity - input grinding, kiln rotation, clinker grinding, and even some dust recovery. In general, the larger the plant, the greater the power input, although the lower will be the unit power input, owing to scale economies in kiln power demands. On the other hand, higher power input, all other things equal, will yield a better product through finer grinding and more even kiln rotation. Finally, mechanization of some processes, such as intraplant materials transport, will also lead to higher power input per ton, this time in substitution for labor. Therefore, increased power consumption per ton of output indicates greater efficiency - it can generally be presumed to save labor and improve quality. Power consumption did increase by 8% per ton between 1950 and 1962 (Spravochnik, p. 843). Per man hour of employment, the rise was much more dramatic, increasing nearly seven-fold between 1950 and 1968 (p. 837).

Labor

Labor productivity rose markedly, as shown in Table 6.4. The more than ninefold increase since 1928 reflects many factors. First, the product mix has altered in the direction of blends, the 1968 mix including 64% portland (Liusov, p. 9). But a 60% portland mix already characterized output in the mid-30s (see Table 6.1) and productivity has increased about 6-8 times since then. It is also startling that output per man doubled between 1958 and 1968 even while portland was increasing in importance from 45% to 64%. This increase may be exaggerated, however. On the other hand, even if the portland share was unchanged, the average grade over the period was rising regularly by 50% between 1940 and 1967, and by 12% between 1960 and 1967 (Budnikov and Volkonskii, p. 15).

The sources of this growth are undoubtedly the technological factors we have already seen - longer kilns, expansion of gas use, and increased provision of electric power. The larger plant size is surely itself a factor, but it is difficult to separate out the effect of size from the effect of other aspects of technological change. In 1962, according to the cement production handbook, output per man in million-ton plants was twice as high as that in 200,000-350,000 ton plants, but the larger plants were also newer and reflected the most recent technological advances.

Standards

Everything so far considered testifies to a rational industry in the postwar period. Progress in technology has been seen in kiln size, fuel mix, use of electric power, and plant scale. The journals in this period contain abundant evidence of experimentation - on the plant sites and not just in central laboratories - with other improvements such as more efficient heat transfer apparatus and chimney design modification to reduce stack loss. To be sure, in the absence of hard data one could argue that these improvements were not unqualifiedly efficient, that for example, cement is so cheap to produce that it does not pay to install dust loss reduction apparatus, or that power is mispriced and

TABLE 6.4. Annual Output of Hydraulic Cement per Man, 1928-1968, Selected Years

	Tons	1950=100
1928	104	36
1934	138	48
1940	222	77
1950	288	100
1955	535	186
1957	576	200
1958	650	226
1959	681	236
1960	765	266
1961	824	286
1962	877	305
1963	902	313
1964	974	338
1965	1,035	360
1966	1,138	392
1967	1,232	428
1968	1,274	443
1976 *	2,036	708

* Estimate based on total building materials industry output per man.

Sources: 1938-1955, Loginov, 1959, p. 111; 1957-68, Smekhov, p. 3; and Narkhoz, 1977, p. 182.

really represented an inefficient use of resources, but the burden of proof would be on any one advancing this thesis. On the other hand, one unqualified source of inefficiency in the postwar period, as in the 1930s, is the approach to cement standards.

Portland cement standardization methodology in most advanced industrial countries allows for much less strength variability than the Soviet approach. For example, although United States portland cement standards permit five types of portland cement, most variations relate to mineralogical tolerances for use in special conditions or for early hardening (ASTM, p. 3). General purpose (Types I and II) account for around 95% of total production in 1968. This makes it much easier to control output (indeed, as Machlup has argued, this uniformity was a result of the oligopolistic market structure) (1949, p. 80).

According to information presented in Cement Standards of the World, a recent publication of the European Cement Association, uniformity rather than diversity appears to be the rule in most nations. In general, the approach of countries such as the United Kingdom, Japan, Germany, or Brazil is to have one basic or ordinary type, supplemented by special purpose types (early-hardening, low-heat, sulfate-resistant). Nothing is seen that resembles the Soviet practice of permitting five or six grades of ordinary portland, to be decided by test, in addition to specially marked early-hardening cement, and those with special mineralogical properties. The Soviet practice is to grade the cement as it leaves the kilns. The grade distribution is shown in Table 6.5.

TABLE 6.5. Grade Mix of Hydraulic Cements
            1962 and 1965, Percent of Total

| Grade | 1962 | | | | 1976 |
	Portland	Portland Pozzolan	Portland - Slag	Total	Total
200					1.6
300	1.7	3.1	29.3	11.1	17.4
400	22.4	48.4	53.6	35.8	60.5
500	63.1	47.7	17.1	44.6	18.5
600 and higher	12.7	.8	-	6.7	3.2
Total	100.0	100.0	100.0	98.2	98.4

Sources: 1962 Spravochnik. pp. 836-839; Narkhoz, 1977, p. 239.

There are four advantages in a uniform standards system, with a reasonably high strength requirement: lower production costs; lower transport and attendant costs; greater reliability; and easier plant performance measurement and control.

Lower production costs

The most complete analysis of the relationship between quality and production cost was given by A. Evdokimenko of the Moscow sovnarkhoz in 1965. His calculations show that the production cost of grade 700 is about 16% higher than grade 400, although its concrete making potential is nearly 50% greater! Its cost is 5% higher than grade 500, while its concrete potential is 17% greater (pp. 5-6).

Thus, in the first place, imposition of higher strength requirements would have sharply reduced concrete-making costs on this account.

Transport and related costs

If grade 700 has 50% greater concrete making potential, only 2/3 ton would have to be shipped for every ton of grade 400 that it replaced. For the prewar period, the transport overexpenditure on this count was estimated to be 28% of total transport cost. The relative transport overexpenditure was probably of the same order in the postwar period. Excess production cost was around 6%, and probably about the same in the postwar period. The total relative inefficiency in the industry today is less, however, perhaps around 10%, since transport costs bulk smaller today.

In addition, however, related savings would have arisen through better shipping practices. For the prewar period, it was estimated that dust loss may have resulted in a cost of 10% when cement was shipped in bulk, which was the case for about 2/3 of total shipments. Losses in the postwar period have been variously estimated at 3% on four important rail lines including the Volga and Ukraine networks (Loginov, 1957, Ch. 4), and as high as 8-10 million tons from all causes in distribution in 1968 (Kobrin and Liusov, p. 1).

The last estimate amounts to 10% of that year's production, and, if true, is astounding. The estimate is accompanied by an attempt to relate the losses to different kinds of rolling stock. The internal consistency of the various loss information in the article, together with the apparent care in analyzing transport-related costs (cleaning of wagons, loading and unloading, etc.), seems to support the 8-10 million ton loss estimate.

Reliability

What has so far been said argues for raising product strength, not necessarily for product uniformity. We would maintain, however, that if the wisdom of holding to the multi-grade system of cement standards had been reviewed, a single high grade would have been adopted which would then have justified construction of specialized rolling stock. (Bags were not really the answer since they require extensive and costly handling.) But the very fact of uniformity would itself have had a positive influence on the industry.

Now, the problem of reliability in construction is never explicitly analyzed in the cement industry journals, but certainty regarding grade must have been a serious problem for builders. In the first place, builders frequently had to deal blindly with cement since it was often shipped in advance of the 28-day test specifications, which were sent as they became available. As one author put it in 1954, "Usually, by the time the user gets the test documents, the cement has already been used, so that he is unable to get full value from it" (Pomiluiko, p. 24). It was urged that this practice be terminated in 1964, ("Uluchshat'....", p. 1), and the situation had not improved by 1968. According to a check by Gossnab in that year "cement is used in construction in far from optimal ways" (Kravchenko et al., p.5). Indeed research to develop procedures for accelerated testing and early prediction of 28-day test strengths is a recurring theme in Tsement.

Finally, the multiplicity of grades wrought chaos in some of the warehousing installations. With a possible total of 30. or 40 grade-types to store, (4) there must have been a great deal of confusion. For example, according to Kravchenko et al. (p. 5):

Trust No. 4 of Glavvolgoviatskstroi (in Dzerzhinsk) receives ten different kinds and grades from six suppliers, while even the largest concrete-making plant has only four cement storage silos, as a rule. In these circumstances, different grades of cement will inevitably get mixed up, and cement is bound to be used as though it were all the lower grade, resulting in substantial losses of this building material.

It goes without saying, of course, that any attempt to raise exports would require better grading procedures. One plant (Novorossiissk), for example, seeking export markets advertises its product as all being equal to British standard, which shows an awareness of the advantages of a single grade system. (5)

Measurement and control

Grade multiplicity makes it extremely difficult to control and measure performance. For example, how should the performance of the two hypothetical plants with output as shown in Table 6.6 be compared? How should performance be calculated? How should it be related to production cost? Evdokimenko in the previously cited 1964 article proposed conversion coefficients expressed in terms of concrete-making capacity, but the idea, though seconded by some others, has never caught on. In any event, such coefficients neglect the very important dimension of transport input, i.e., that 1½ tons of grade 400, which are nominally equal to one ton of grade 700 in terms of concrete-making potential, would require 50% more transport to do the same job.

The easiest solution to the control and performance evaluation problem is to impose a single-grade standards policy. Considering the manifest superiority of this approach, especially for a planned economy, it is little short of incredible that the issue has been so little discussed. Many of the difficulties inherent in the present system have, of course, been recognized, as is evident from the foregoing allusions.

TABLE 6.6.   Hypothetical Product Mix of Two Plants

Yearly Production by

	Plant A		Plant B	
Grade	Tons	Percent of total	Tons	Percent of total
300	50	14.3	60	17.1
400	110	31.4	90	25.7
500	80	22.8	70	20.0
600	60	17.1	70	20.0
700	50	14.3	60	17.1
Total	350	100.0	350	100.0

Development of conversion coefficients based on concrete-making capacity has been proposed by a number of other writers as well. (6) One of these writers (Vezlomtsev) on another occasion proposed a more Marxist approach, recommending a production cost rather than use-value criterion (Vezlomtsev, pp. 8-9).   The system, which had been developed by the Scientific Research Institute for Cement (NIITsement), and was ready for use, commensurated all grades in terms of their labor content, labor being the best indicator of prime cost. The trouble with use-value coefficients, according to Vezlomtsev, was that there were scale economies - unit and materials, fuel, power, and labor costs all fall with rising strength (calculated either by standard 28-day tests or concrete-making capacity) - and so these indicators fail to be an accurate index of the cost of production.   This is true, of course; they do not.   But institution of the NIITsement system of indicators would give no incentive to higher quality - indeed, it might serve as a disincentive. The plant would be guided by the relationship between the labor ratio and the total cost ratio of different grades or types, and there is no way to tell whether this relationship would stimulate higher quality. For example, suppose that the patterns shown in Table 6.7 held for portland 400 and portland 600 (per ton):

TABLE 6.7. Hypothetical Comparison of Production Inputs

	Labor input	Total production cost/rubles	Concrete-making capacity (grade 400=100)
400	3.0	30	100
600	3.2	35	131
Ratio	1.07	1.16	1.31

It is easy to show that in this case the result would be perverse. Thus, the advantage to the national economy from producing the higher grade is the improved concrete-making strength divided by the increased production cost, or $(1.3/1.16)-1 = 12.9\%$. The higher grade is, therefore, more efficient. Commensurating output in terms of labor cost, however, would mean that if the plant produced the higher grade, it would have to spend 8.4% more per unit of its success indicator. That is, it would spend 16% more and raise its success indicator by only 8.4%, and so it would produce the lower grade.

That negligence of grade uniformity has continued so long is the more difficult to understand, since Soviet technicians have long been familiar with international testing procedures and product specifications. Numerous comparative tests and specifications presented in Tsement in the last two decades attest to this. Perhaps part of the problem is that these publications place too much stress on the diversity rather than uniformity of some foreign products. For example, in 1959 and again in 1965, (7) tables are presented which show the five types of United States portland cement, giving them equal prominence and suggesting, thereby, that they are all approximately equal in the industry's output. The fact is never mentioned that 94% of total output (in 1968) is Type I and II - ordinary general purpose and ordinary low heat portlands, with the same strength characteristics but differing slightly in mineralogical composition - and that the others are produced in small quantities (about 6% in all) for special purposes, as indicated by their name, e.g., rapid-hardening, sulfate-resistant, etc. (8)

CONCLUSION

In this chapter we have reviewed three approaches to the analysis of economic efficiency in industry - behavioral-anecdotal analysis, productivity analysis based on aggregate production functions, and empirical analysis of the technological adaptation of individual industries. The first approach frequently fails to take account of factors which act as checks and balances, and that analyses based on the second approach tend to overlook all of the implications of the method. Empirical studies show, however, that total factor productivity has been on the order of 2-3%, which constitutes a creditable enough performance by Western standards. We remind the reader of the two main reservations that must be expressed to such studies: 1) if any positive total factor productivity is measured, an underlying organizational weakness in the economy is implied, as we discussed above; and 2) this does not bear on Pareto efficiency, but only on growth. In other words, the charge could still be leveled that the Pareto-efficient rate of growth would have involved a higher rate of technical change or total factor productivity. More generally, to be Pareto-efficient - to be able to increase output of some industries or commodities only by reducing that of others - cannot be inferred from studies of factor productivity. The same objections, of course, would apply to this type of analysis in the West. But if the latter are accepted, so should those for the Soviet economy. The conclusion, in view of the studies just cited, therefore, is that the economy has performed well.

Finally, the analysis of individual industries. There have not been as many studies of individual industries or of sufficient depth as would be desirable to make statements about the efficiency of industry in general. The one industry reviewed here does support the view that industry is reasonably efficient, its postwar performance and organization being deficient only in the formulation of product standards. It could be argued, of course, that we chose the cement industry for analysis precisely because it is marked by a number of critical and relatively unambiguous indicators of performance, and by concentrating on these we could see whether the industry has been headed in the right direction. This being the case, we might also expect the managers in this industry themselves to be able to cope more satisfactorily than managers in more complex industries, such as chemicals or machinery. There may be some truth in this, and apart from urging that further work be done, there is little to do at the moment for the analysis of all industry through individual industry studies. One other approach, however, is to analyze the operating rules of the economy and see whether these are such as would stimulate efficiency. In Chapter 7 we analyze the information necessary for implementing of what could be the most important rules - the information provided by the economy's price mechanism.

NOTES

(1) Calculated from Narkhoz, 1977, pp. 20, 205, 208, 212, and 239, and Narkhoz, 1972, p. 169.

(2) Soviet hydraulic cements are divided into three classes: 1) portland cement, ground from clinker, produced by roasting calcium carbonate and silicious materials in a kiln, and then grinding; 2) portland pozzolan, produced by grinding portland clinker together with 20-50% (of final weight) pozzolanic (volcanic) materials, not cementitious themselves, but capable of reacting with lime to form a hydraulic binder; and 3) portland-slag cement, formed by grinding portland clinker with blast furnace slag (20-85% of final weight), which contains silica and lime, and reacts with the portland to form a permanent binder. The portland specification itself permits the introduction of additives (up to 15% by final product weight). There are also various special purpose cements (oil-well, white and colored portland cements, aluminous cement etc.)

(3) Asbestos-cement shingle production in the mid-70s was around 7.5 billion standard units per year (Narkhoz, 1978, p. 241).

(4) There were 35 in 1963, and new grades were being added or dropped. New standards, applying primarily to testing procedures, were introduced in 1966. ("Uluchshat'...")

(5) Tsement, 1966, No. 4, Advertisement on back cover.

(6) E.g., Loginov, Tsem. prom., p. 245. Slightly different coefficients, based on the same principle, are proposed by S.I. Il'in and V.I. Vezlomtsev, "Planirovat' proizvodztvo i potreblenie tsementa s uchetom ego kachestva," Tsement, 1963, No. 5, p. 6.

(7) "Standarty razlichnykh stran na portlandtsement," Tsement, 1959, No. 5, pp. 23-24; B.V. Volkonskii and N.P. Shteiert, "Rol' standartov v povyshenii kachestva tsementa," Tsement, 1965, No. 3, pp. 1-3.

(8) Minerals Yearbook, Vol. I-II, 1968, p. 259, U.S. Bureau of Mines, Department of the Interior, Washington. The Bureau reports Types I and II together. Both are for general use. But the latter is especially suited to use under moderate sulfate action or where low heat of hydration is required. It has different mineralogical specifications which are imposed. Types III, IV, and V are for high early strength, low heat of hydration, and high sulfate resistance. There are in addition various types of air-entraining cements. All of these, small amounts of portland-slag and portland pozzolan, and other special purpose mixes accounted for 6% of production in 1968.

7 The Price Mechanism and Economic Efficiency

The extensive complexities that arise when we analyze the behavior and efficiency of an industry, sector, or whole economy lead us to try an indirect approach: look at the operating rules of the economy or sector and, from these, try to reach conclusions regarding the efficiency of that sector or economy. Since inevitably these rules involve the price mechanism, implicitly or explicitly, or assumptions about its functioning, we now turn to this topic.

Our main concern is to examine the socialist price system from the viewpoint of its ability to promote efficient production decisions. Since a price system also serves other ends - conditioning the distribution of income and also serving to measure output, to use the valuable distinctions emphasized by Morris Bornstein (1966) - we must not lose sight of the question whether the price system is consistent as well as efficient, i.e., whether it can consistently serve all of the important functions which it is called upon to serve.

Now, observers have often argued that, even disregarding the issue of consistency, the Soviet price mechanism is hopelessly perverse and incapable of promoting efficiency, principally because it is based on Marxian precepts about the labor theory of value - in addition, it is sometimes reasoned that this perversity reflects the inherent inability of any bureaucracy to devise rational prices. Since such criticisms presume that prices in a capitalist market economy are effective in serving these ends, we begin this chapter with a short section questioning this conventional view. We see that, both in the capitalist model of pure theory and in the actual Western capitalist market economy, there are many shortcomings which are too often allowed to fade beyond our analytical horizons or go entirely unrecognized.

Following the analysis of the market economy, we turn to the Soviet price system, considering especially the two defects which are most important from the viewpoint of Western analysis, namely its alleged failure to incorporate differential rent premia in prices and its failure to allow for a capital charge. We will examine the validity of these claims, primarily from the viewpoint of efficiency, but keeping consistency in mind as well. The analysis in this chapter will show that the case is not nearly so clear cut as has so often been supposed by Western observers, and that there is no reason for believing that the West inevitably generates a sounder price system than that in the Soviet socialist economy.

SOME PROBLEMS IN THE CAPITALIST PRICE SYSTEM

On the basis of propositions about economic self-interest and competition in a capitalist economy we have traditionally deduced certain features which must characterize prices and the price system, and then made further conclusions about the efficiency of the behavior of participants in the economy. The usual conclusion is that capitalist organization and performance are efficient, that the capitalist economy is still led by the "invisible hand" that Adam Smith first postulated 200 years ago. We usually do concede that the assumptions regarding perfect competition are somewhat exaggerated and that the hand, if not arthritic, has at least lost some of its vigor, that without a bit of ointment from time to time it may not lead always and everywhere to a social optimum. But most economists and observers are fairly satisfied that it works pretty well most of the time.

When we do investigate more closely, however, the characteristics of the price mechanism even in a theoretical Western, perfectly competitive model - not to mention an actually existing economy, such as the United States - we really must question these conclusions more severely than is our wont. The defects are much more widespread and much more varied than we are accustomed to think they are. The objections most often raised to the price mechanism in such capitalist economies are based on monopoly pricing practices and, since many writers have shown that the shortfalls from efficiency thereby occasioned are small, maybe the invisible hand is performing well after all. But this is only one of the defects of the price mechanism in the capitalist market economy. We will consider three other types of imperfection which may at times be more subtle and may result from behind-the-scenes maneuvering, but which constitute a serious obstacle to economic efficiency. (They also frequently have an undesirable effect on the distribution of income as well.) The three defects we will consider are: 1) the inability of the market to ensure that the price correctly reflects all the demands for a product, including future demands. This defect is exemplified most notably today by the prices of fossil fuels, 2) the failure to ensure that prices in regulated industries correctly reflect incremental social costs; and 3) the inability or unwillingness to ensure that prices of many services in the public sector correctly reflect the cost structure of the activity. We will briefly consider examples of these three problems.

1) Inability to determine and/or incorporate the true economic rent to reflect all demands for a commodity: This is nowhere better exemplified than by the inability of the market to determine the correct price for crude oil (not to speak of the ability of the market to put such a price into practice, given the political and economic vested interests generated by the system in the first place). Now, the price of crude oil should allow for a premium or economic rent over the cost of production (except, possibly, for new high-cost deposits, which are induced into production only by the existence of a high rent-inclusive price). The price of a commodity is supposed to reflect the demand for that commodity, which in turn reflects its advantages as an inter-mediate or final consumption good. This is true not only for crude oil, but also for competing fuels as well as competing chemical feed stocks. For example, the premium should reflect the cost saving or social advantage generated by using this input rather than something else: the premium for high-grade coal over low-grade coal; the premium for gas, relative to its cost of production, over coal; the premium for oil over the cost of producing the best alternative fuel and also the crude oil price premium or rent simultaneously reflects the greater utility in use and/or cost savings when petroleum derivatives are used for other products, such as chemical fertilizers, plastic mixing bowls, and so on. Now, while it is an act of faith to imagine that production patterns do adjust until the correct premiums are established, simultaneously ensuring equilibrium in all these markets and uses in the short term, it is much more difficult to imagine that intertemporal equilibrium is also achieved. How can we ensure that the premium for a resource also reflects the cost being imposed on a future user by the early exhaustion of that resource? The premium is supposed to ration resources in such a way as to ensure that the value received by anybody using a unit of that resource is at least as great as the cost that he will impose on someone else by making that resource unavailable to him. While it may be theoretically possible to do this in the short term, it is still improbable; but it is not even theoretically possible in the long run because of the uncertainty concerning future technological developments and resource availabilities.

When it comes to the real-world Western capitalist economy, the picture is much worse. Not only do we observe situations in which the long-term rent premium does not arise spontaneously to be incorporated in a price but even in the short term, with fixed resources, such rents are not automatically incorporated in prices. Consider again the recent developments in the world petroleum market. With prices of ten to twelve dollars a barrel in some regions of the world, we have prices of six or eight dollars in North America for domestic production. This encourages people to use oil for less urgent needs. If the world price is twelve dollars, and North America is pricing it internally at six dollars, domestic oil is being used up frivolously: it could be sold for the world market price of twelve dollars - if not today, then tomorrow. Or as an input into the production of commodities that enter world trade, a higher oil price would dictate a higher final price, again earning better returns. The ramifications are broad and deep: inefficient gasoline-intensive urban transport and inefficient residential patterns are encouraged; products using petroleum as a raw material or as an energy input are priced too low, with the result that inefficient domestic consumption patterns are encouraged. All this happens, essentially, because marginal valuations or utilities are equated to prices which are less than the incremental costs which, in turn, reflect regulated opportunities, thus contradicting a feature long held to be the unequalled glory of the capitalist price system!

2) Failure of regulated industries to reflect true incremental social cost: Part of the capitalist catechism is that the price mechanism leads to zero profits, implying that nobody earns excess income. From this it also follows that income distribution is not grossly out of line with the dictates of efficiency: as you sow, so shall you reap; increase income by working harder, selling more, etc.

However, the difficulty is that zero-profit criterion is only valid for small businesses in the unregulated economy. In the regulated economy, which is regulated in the first place as an antidote to the presumed consequences of monopoly that would otherwise follow, zero profits may mean any of three things: a) the firm is operating efficiently; b) the firm is operating inefficiently in the sense of exercising too little control over the expenditure of resources while the regulatory authority is hard put to question the cost record presented to it for rating purposes; or c) salaries are extremely high and, since it is usually a simple matter to build them into the cost which serves the regulatory authority as a basis for pricing, we do find zero profits but in no meaningful sense can we speak of the pervasiveness of zero excess income! The numerous cases of this type of tolerance by regulatory authorities in recent years speak for themselves.

3) Irrational pricing in the public sector: Richard Musgrave (1959) has distinguished three major reasons for performing activities in the public sector, viz., promotion of efficiency, stabilization, and income distribution. Accordingly, there are three types of influence on public sector pricing policies, one of which has unambiguous implications for the relationship of price of cost (income distribution) while others do not. We have argued elsewhere (1977c) that it is not possible to give general rules for the pricing of activities undertaken for purposes of efficiency, sometimes the price being charged is properly below incremental ascribable cost, and sometimes not. One of the problems in framing such a rule is to decide what is the incremental ascribable cost.

In the work cited we have argued that the area where incremental costs can be determined and imposed, in a manner which is much more efficient than is frequently supposed, is really rather broad. But many interest groups hide behind slick public relations obfuscation and, at times, "sound economic analysis," to avoid paying such prices. Thus, "This truck pays $6,000 a year in fuel and license taxes," we read as we choke on the exhaust of the 30-ton tractor-semi in front of us. The implied accusation of "How much do you pay?" makes us squirm uncomfortably, while we neglect entirely to ask back "How much should you be paying?" and are ill-equipped to think about devising a procedure for allocating cost. Unfortunately, the truckers' lobby thrives on ignorance and few people have any information about average annual run by vehicle size, load, etc., or, worse, few people even know what the basic relationship between size and damage is - even many respectable economists assume that all vehicles are equal in their damage per mile. In reality the damage imposed is an exponential function of vehicle size, with the damage coefficient typically increasing about 10-20 fold as we double the axle load. According to the major empirical study (AASHO, 1962), the damage coefficient of a modest size truck is 800 times that of a car, so clearly the big trucks should pay much more than small trucks of cars for the reconstruction part of the annual highway budget. What is the situation? It is not at all clear, in the United States the highway trust fund draws on gasoline taxes wherever generated, including those from cities where such taxes might be justified as an income distribution charge or as a congestion control device, but should certainly not be earmarked for the interstate highway system so there is some presumption big trucks do not contribute appropriately to highway reconstruction costs.

In Europe the tradition is followed of "proving" that the public provision for highways is efficiently priced since total income of the road sector is equal to expenses on investment, maintenance, and administration. Unfortunately, "income" as calculated includes sales taxes, most of which are more properly viewed as a revenue raising or income distribution device and should not be included as payment for use of roads. Moreover, it would be small satisfaction to know that equality existed if it were achieved only by having cars pay much more and trucks much less than their own directly ascribable incremental cost - i.e., not the average cost for all users but that cost which can definitely be ascribed to class. The only country for which a study of road user charges has been done that makes use of the AASHO coefficients is the author's study of Yugoslavia (1974) in which, curiously, it was concluded that in the variant of the socialist economy, road pricing was unexpectedly rational.

THE SOVIET PRICE MECHANISM

For the first two decades of its existence, technical controversy about the workability of the Soviet economy centered on its ability to generate prices which could serve as correct signals for economic decisions. The controversy was a series of small steps forward, with a new obstacle being proposed by a conservative, market-oriented skeptic each time that one was cleared by the socialist opposition, until finally Oskar Lange in the 1930s seemed to solve the problem. He presented a simulation substitute for the freely functioning market of the capitalist world to determine prices that could generate efficiency. (1) What this solution did, essentially, was to offer the same guidelines for making production decisions as in the capitalist world, at least in the short term. It is not usually noted that this solution really had little to say about how the overall decisions about allocation of output between consumption and investment were to be made, or which industries were to be emphasized, etc. To cite this shortcoming is not to imply that the Western capitalist economy does make these decisions correctly; but neither should we be misled about just what the so-called Lange-Taylor solution does or does not do.

Efficient solution of the longer-term problems which the Lange-Taylor market-economy simulation guidelines could not handle would be promoted or even guaranteed if prices could be made to reflect correctly the intertemporal substitution possibilities of economic resources. This would require the incorporation of economic rents, including "rent" for capital, a function performed in the West by the rate of interest (although not performed efficiently, it has been argued by many writers). (2) But in the socialist system it is argued that rent in this broader sense, i.e., including the rent for capital, is assumed to be proscribed by Marx.

To analyze the question whether the Soviet price mechanism is deficient because it subscribes to Marx, we must proceed in stages, asking the following questions:

What does Marx really say about differential rent and capital charges?

Is the Soviet price system nominally based on Marx? If it is and if Marx does preclude the use of such instruments, is it possible that the Soviet price system may have evolved mechanisms which do perform the functions of differential rent and capital charges anyway?

Finally, but last only in order of presentation, how desirable are the instruments of economic rent and interest from the general point of view, taking into account all the functions which the price mechanism must serve, including promotion of static or short-term efficiency, dynamic or intertemporal efficiency, and income distribution goals? (3)

None of these questions has an easy answer. Even concerning what Marx said, for example, most of us taught to associate Marx with the labor theory of value - the notion that all value derives from and can be measured by the amount of labor entering a commodity - must be astonished at the following passage in a recent article in Ekonomika i matemachiskie metody, by N.Ia. Petrakov (1974) who goes further than anyone to date in asserting the pre-eminence of Marx as a utilitarian. Those of his disciples who insisted on a strict labor-cost-of-production approach Petrakov relegates to the intellectual scrap-heap of history along with Ricardo and Smith, on the one hand, and along with those who overstressed utility, on the other. The paper is remarkable for its absolute conviction:

These words are heard today with great urgency. They might have been especially intended by Engels for economists who in recent years have set enthusiastically to the task of calculating labor time and who attempt by these means to adjust the price system. Direct and full labor costs are calculated, and comparisons between levels of labor content and prices in different sectors of the national economy are compared. From these comparisons numerous conclusions are derived about deviations between prices and labor norms. But what does it mean, for example, to show that the price for chemical products, calculated according to labor norms, is twice as high, or, conversely, half as high as the currently existing price? What practical actions should be undertaken on the basis of such information (Petrakov, p. 671).

Lest we think that this is merely the work of a Soviet economist of the new school, impatient to apply his mathematical formulations and multipliers to planning practice, let Marx speak for himself. The impasse that he inevitably reached when adapting theoretical simplifications to the complexities of the real world of labor input measurement is illustrated in the following quotation from A Critique of the Gotha Programme, written in 1875:

In spite of this advance, this equal right is still perpetually burdened with a bourgeois limitation. The right of the producers is proportional to the labour they supply; the equality consists in the fact that measurement is made with an equal standard, labour. But one man is superior to another physically or mentally and so supplies more labour in the same time, or can work for a longer time; and labour, to serve as a measure, must be defined by its duration or intensity, otherwise it ceases to be a standard of measurement. This equal right is an unequal right for unequal labour. It recognizes no class differences, because everyone is only a worker like everyone else; but it tacitly recognizes unequal individual endowment and thus productive capacity of the worker as natural privileges. It is, therefore, a right of inequality, in its content, like every right. Right by its very nature can consist only in the application of an equal standard; but unequal individuals (and they would not be different individuals if they were not unequal) are measurable only by the same standard in so far as they are brought under the same point of view, are taken from one definite side only, for instance, in the present case, are regarded only as workers, and nothing more is seen in them, everything else being ignored. Further, one worker is married, another not; one has more children than another, and so on and so forth. Thus, with an equal performance of labour, and hence an equal share in the social consumption fund, one will in fact receive more than another, one will be richer than another, and so on. To avoid all these defects, right instead of being equal would have to be unequal (pp. 16-17).

Thus, the question of what Marx really said and what he really meant is moot. Moreover, it is not possible to define a single statement on which all Soviet planners and ideologues have agreed since the beginning or have agreed even at any single time. Many thoughtful observers, most recently Francis Seton (1977) for example, have concluded that Marxian belief is not inconsistent with rational price setting.

It is difficult to state an overall consensus regarding the principles of price formation, whether existing now or at any one time, or even what official effective Soviet policy on these matters is. Yet it is significant that in its most recent version, the Great Soviet Encyclopedia does allow a place in price formation for economic rent for both resources and capital (BSE, 1970). Even in the previous edition, rent was allowed for natural resources and land. We hasten to add that merely to allow a premium or rent does not ensure that the correct amount would be determined and used, any more than it can be assumed to be included automatically in capitalist price formation, as we observed earlier in this chapter. When surcharges for actual harm done the economy as well as the mere drawing down of resources is considered, there is very little hope that the price for any resource serves simultaneously to balance all of the considerations discussed above. That is, harm done the environment by extraction, cost imposed on a second user of this resource by the first firm's use, cost imposed upon the user of a completely different resource by the use of the first firm, cost or disutility imposed upon a consumer by the unavailability of this resource for his need because it is used for another's need, and cost imposed upon a future generation's use because of use today. We neither can nor should expect the price mechanism in the Soviet economy to be more successful in performing this function than that in a capitalist economy. But this should not blind us to the possibility, and the fact, that attempts are being made to approach pricing from this point of view.

Keeping in mind this diversity of constraints and influences on the development of rents should also help us to appreciate the fact that rents which may be correct for some functions may be inappropriate for others. For example, rents which may be correct from the viewpoint of short-term resource allocation may be inappropriate for long-term efficiency, and also inappropriate from the viewpoint of more equal income distribution.

Besides recognizing this multifunctional quality of rents, any real world analysis must consider the possibility that the economy may have evolved surrogate measures to perform any or all of these functions. From this, let us look at the functioning of capital charges and natural resource rents in the Soviet economy.

ANALYSIS OF SOVIET CAPITAL CHARGES

A capital charge is supposed to promote better use of existing equipment and efficient decisions about new investment. We refer to the former as short-term efficiency and the latter as long-term efficiency. We will see that the Soviet economy has evolved short-term capital changes over the years in a way which is not inconsistent with Marx since, in the first place, there is some ambiguity or room for manuever in Marx, as noted above. This short-term charge is based on industry wage differentials which are not themselves based on reproduction costs and which also work to ensure that labor is directed to its most effective utilization. The long-term capital charge, for which we in the West seek some sort of counterpart corresponding to the rate of interest on a bond, need not be incorporated into the price of capital, however. As we will see, the Soviet economy has developed criteria for determining what projects to invest in and these are not at all in conflict with Marxian doctrine. Marx really leaves unanswered many of the issues for which these criteria are used.

Any existing capital good - a machine, a plant, or any other input to production which represents the previous embodiment of labor- must be used efficiently. Since at a given point in time there will probably be more people wanting to use capital . equipment than there will be equipment available, the equipment must be rationed. One way to ration is through administrative fiat, which is cumbersome since it requires that a central administrator have at this disposal a vast quantity of information. An alternative method for rationing is the price mechanism - setting prices for the equipment which will ensure that its use is given first to those willing to pay the most. But the willingness of users to pay will be conditioned primarily by the savings in direct labor that the machine permits them to reap; for example, a mining firm will be willing to pay for the use of an excavator an amount which depends on the labor saving, measured in money, that the firm achieves by using the machine. This amount will not in general be equal to the amount of labor time that went into the production of the machine. But since according to Marx it is this labor time that determines or causes value, which should equal price, a Marx-based price for the excavator will fail to serve as an efficient rationing device for labor. Hence, any price system based on Marx will be inefficient, given the conventional argument.

Before this conclusion can be accepted, we must look more carefully at the actual way prices have come to be formed historically. In accordance with the comments above, a capital charge or interest for short-term decisions is the productivity differential of capital over labor. But it also follows that any output will be priced according to the labor intensity and capital intensity of the inputs into its production. Capital intensity is defined by prices which include this productivity differential. Such a definition, of course, opens the possibility that a productivity differential may exist which is not explicitly added to the output price or explicitly referred to as a capital charge or interest. May such differentials actually exist in the Soviet economy? Indeed there are differentials and always have been since the Soviet Union started on the planned route to industrialization. These have taken the form of the differentiated wages that were instituted in the 1930s, although the precise amounts of the differentials may not have corresponded exactly to the productivity differentials that the rationalist would like them to equal.

In the Soviet mode of reckoning, the costs of capital goods and consumer goods may be resolved entirely into labor cost. How is labor cost itself to be measured? The common practice is to treat the wage bill as the labor cost for any industry. But the wage in capital equipment industries already contains a premium as compared with the wage in consumption-goods industries, this premium apparently exceeding the cost of producing the labor itself. Bergson gives an example of a cashier's wage differential of 89% between the meat processing and nonferrous metals industries (1964, p. 117). More generally, as Aganbegian and Maier have shown (1959), industrial variation in average wages has been very wide, and this appears due to causes other than labor reproduction cost. That the capital-goods industries and those producing primarily for their support have been favored with high wage incentives is generally agreed. This conscious wage policy is evident in the tremendous transformation in the ranking of industries which accompanied the five-year plans. For example, according to Aganbegian and Maier, only three of the nine industries that ranked highest in average wage in 1956 were among the nine highest in 1924. The four highest in 1956 - coal, iron mining, steel, and petroleum - ranked 10, 15, 13, and 11 in 1924 and 14, 12, 9, and 8 in 1928 (p. 190).

The force behind the radical change in interindustry wage structure was undoubtedly the competition for workers in the 1930s, with wages in Soviet industry rising by nearly 400% during the 1930s. Officials were unable to stem the tide. As Holzman has put it (1960, p. 176):

> True, wages were set by the state; but these scales presented no obstacle to wage inflation because of the widespread upgrading, illegitimate use of bonus money, and other such devices. The labor market was in such a turmoil that in 1930, for example, workers in large scale industry changed jobs, on the average, more than one and one-half times a year.

With firms in such a situation it was natural that those receiving a greener go-ahead signal from the top, i.e., heavy industry, would outbid the traditional industries, leading to the change in rankings observed by Aganbegian and Maier.

That the practice has been institutionalized and obtains today is shown most clearly in the quotation from E.I. Kapustin already cited on page 16. Additional support for this thesis is provided by Leonard Kirsch (1972) who concludes (p. 174) that

> Soviet economists simply hold that the initial basic rate (of an industry) should be further adjusted for a branch's importance or its expected growth so that certain industries are "first in line" in hiring additional workers.

What is the significance of these wage comparisons and comments? (4) They are very persuasive evidence that the prices of capital goods, if based simply on the labor costs of the input components as measured by wages, do already contain a premium over the labor cost of production which can serve as an interest charge or rent on scarce capital.

For the sake of illustration consider the following hypothetical example shown in Table 7.1. The nonferrous metals industry is assumed to have an average wage 90% higher than the average food industry wage (Aganbegian and Maier, 1959, p. 187). Suppose that half of this difference is due to greater training requirements and other factors influencing the reproduction cost of labor, while half constitutes an incentive to attract labor to this industry, which the planners wish to favor. Suppose that in one week the food worker produces food valued at 60 rubles (60 kilograms of canned fish, say) while the nonferrous worker produces a capital good valued at 150 rubles, all output valued in terms of wages actually paid, as shown in Table 7.1.

TABLE 7.1. Hypothetical Analysis of Price-Labor Cost Relationship

	Nonferrous metals industry	Food Industry	
		Production by nonferrous worker if he transferred to food industry	Production by food industry worker
1. Value of output	150	114	60
2. Cost of materials (including capital consumption)	74	38	20
3. Wages	76	58	40
4. Reproduction cost of labor	58	58	40
5. Value added (1-2)	76	76	40
6. Net value added (5-4)	18	18	0

The direct (own industry) labor inputs into food and nonferrous metals are, let us say, 40 and 76 rubles' worth of each man's labor respectively. Now, since the nonferrous worker is a superior worker, one week's work by him, if it were applied in the food industry, would produce, say, 114 rubles of product (114 kilos of canned fish). The opportunity cost of employing this man in nonferrous metals production is, then, 18 rubles, which is the differential net-value-added that he would have created in the food industry (Table 7.1, line 6). We should certainly wish to impute such a charge to the nonferrous industry. Thus, the output of the nonferrous worker in his own industry is priced to reflect both the total wages bill involved in its production (which exceeds the cost of reproducing the labor at all levels going into it) and the opportunity cost of using the worker in that industry rather than the food industry. At the next stage of production, the input of nonferrous metals will already reflect this opportunity cost and yet another may be added, etc.

In the ideal hypothetical example of Table 7.1, the opportunity cost is precisely the amount of the wage incentive in the nonferrous metals industry. Therefore, the price of the capital good based on the wage cost of production is already ample to cover this opportunity cost, and therefore it would be wrong to add another interest imputation. Unfortunately, of course, there is no way to tell how closely this wage premium does in fact correspond to the opportunity cost and, hence, whether an additional interest imputation is required. But in principle it need not be. The Soviet pricemakers can simultaneously be faithful to Marx (base prices on labor cost of production, where labor costs are calculated as the wages paid) and Marshall (with the wages paid incorporating either accidentally or consciously the opportunity cost of using the labor in this, rather than an alternative way).

To summarize, the industry wage premia existing in heavy industry since the mid-30s have played the role of an interest surrogate to raise prices of capital goods relative to labor, and this has worked in the direction of more rational short-term resource allocation in the economy. We have also argued that differentiation of wages was a necessary adjunct to the rapid industrialization which the economy sought, the rapid industrialization itself being an inherent part of the Soviet model - being, indeed, the quintessence of the Soviet approach to development. Accordingly, we would argue that the Soviet economy has generated wage premia which can serve the role which the short-term interest instrument is called upon to play in the West. This does not mean that the industry premia which evolved were necessarily the correct ones. Or to put it another way, in actual circumstances there is no mechanism to ensure that the wage premia that subsequently determine the price of the industry's output will coincide with productivity differentials. But, in principle, there is no reason why they could not.

We turn next to the interest charge for new investment, the long-term allocation of resources to production. The question is, should labor be used to create a capital good which will then be used to produce something in the economy to replace labor in the future? The long-term instrument should be used in a way which is neutral with respect to relative input prices; i.e., it should not impose upon price a further capital charge beyond the short-term productivity differential which, we have argued, is reflected, even if not with complete accuracy, by the industry wage differentials. The proper function of the long-term instrument is to provide a cutoff for selecting projects, which is precisely what the Soviet coefficient of relative effectiveness does. Introducing this tool into planning practice in no way affects prices. It merely relates the output differential to the investment input differential and gives a threshold for choosing the more capital-intensive project.

Now, many years before the decree on the use of the Standard Methodology in 1960 ("Tipovaia metodika," 1960) (5) and also subsequently, although to a lesser extent, there had been general opposition to the use of such an instrument in the Soviet economy on the ground that it resembled an interest rate and was inconsistent with Marxian principles. However, the instrument proposed by the Standard Methodology never was intended to enter the prices of commodities and so does not lead these prices away from values based on the labor cost of reproduction. Therefore, it would be difficult to object to the coefficient on the basis of Marxian value theory. The coefficient simply provides a rule to guide investment decisions. Its consistency with Marxian theory would have to be evaluated on the basis of whether or not it led to production patterns that would be at variance with Marx's views.

It seems safe to say that it would be difficult to infer any ordering of production patterns from Marx's writings; surely this theory of value does not imply any unambiguous rule for determining what sectors, industries, or projects to invest in. However, since an economy must devise some criterion for determining what investments to make, and since it can go only so far on the basis of political criteria, it is almost certain that a criterion such as an internal rate of return would emerge eventually - indeed, the fact that it did emerge in the face of rigid opposition from those who believed themselves orthodox in their commitment to Marxism is perhaps the surest testimonial to this conjecture. At the same time, the fact that this instrument does not enter the price of goods makes the Soviet instrument consistent in principle with both short-term and long-term resource-allocation functions.

(NON-CAPITAL) RESOURCE RENTS

In the West, rents have both allocation and distribution aspects. This is true both of capital equipment, where the rent is termed a capital charge, and also exhaustible and inexhaustible natural resources and land. Thus, the first problem facing anyone who would incorporate a rent into the price of a good or service is to recognize and deal with the consequence that income inequality would increase. Hence, not only is it necessary to find a way to introduce a rent that simultaneously ensures efficient allocation in the short term and in the long term, but also one that does not at the same time introduce too much distributional inequality.   We argued above that in the Western capitalist economy there is no certainty that rents are efficient in both the short and long terms, a theme developed at greater length elsewhere (Abouchar, 1977a), where the consistency between efficiency-related rents and distributional objectives of the economy is also examined.   In the present section we look at the questions of efficiency and consistency of rents under Soviet socialism.

Now, the actual Soviet discussion of the theory of rent is still inchoate. Most discussion centers around the treatment of rent as an income distribution measure, and when efficiency is discussed it is from the viewpoint of a rent which is imposed in the first place for distributional purposes.   Two types of differential rent are distinguished, and no transgression of Marxian doctrine seems to be acknowledged: Differential rent I is associated with differential land productivity and in recent years has been specifically linked to more workable mineral deposits. (The final paragraph of the 1970 Encyclopedia article on differential rent makes this adjustment [BSE, Vol. 8, p. 984].)   Differential rent II is said to result from "the differential productivity of marginal investment: its size and rate increase in a planned manner in conditions of intensification and scientific and technological progress in agriculture; it remains almost wholly within agriculture" (ibid).

The question of incompatibility with Marx is allayed, as it were, by reference to the "planned manner in conditions of intensification and scientific and technological progress," a typical characterization of the socialist state founded upon Marx and Lenin. The main theoretical issue to which observers have directed their attention is the way to transfer the rent to the service of the state, i.e., as an income distribution mechanism, rather than as a signal to decentralize and make the process of resource allocation efficient.   There is, however, some awareness of the question of the effect that incorporation of a rent component into the price has on long-term decisions, and, more importantly, some policy makers have, on occasion and in a very natural fashion, devised pricing schemes which have the effect of encouraging good short-term and long-term operations and decisions.

One of these was the zonally differentiated prices for building materials introduced in the late 1930s. To understand in what respect this was an efficient method of pricing, consider the following problem: Suppose that we can succeed in specifying the correct rent for purposes of short-term efficiency. This may have a positive or negative effect on long-term efficiency. It will have a positive effect insofar as the rent discourages rapid exhaustion of the resource that would result if enterprises were encouraged by lower prices to employ technologies or produce output using the resource in question and were driven, following its exhaustion, to high-cost substitutes. On the other hand, the short-term rent may lead to long-term inefficiency, since planners may not receive correct price signals. For example, suppose there are two ore bodies in two different regions. Suppose that the one in the more populated and industrially more developed region has lower extraction costs per ton but higher costs per ton in terms of standardized output (i.e., considering its mineral content). In this case, the output of the deposit in the new region will earn a rent as the difference between the costs of extracting and transporting it to the old region, and the production cost of the ore in the old region. Including the rent in the price promotes efficient short-term decisions. However, if this rent is included in the pit-head price, planners trying to decide on the location of production facilities using this ore as an input - a long-term decision - will not see the cost advantage of this aspect of their operations, since the price they will be faced with will be higher than the rent-exclusive cost. What has been said for the raw material resource also applies to products with large material inputs.

We have mentioned the zonal price system for building materials as one possible example of reconciling the two interests. Under the zonal policy the nation was divided into a number of zones, each of which was characterized by a single price for a given grade of cement. Cement users anywhere in a given zone would pay the same price for the material. This price would have to cover the cost of production plus the cost of transporting the cement to the zone and to the given construction site or builder's warehouse. The zonal price principally reflected the production costs in that zone, so that it would have the effect of enabling all users to be evaluated in their performance on the same basis, i.e., not giving an edge to any construction firm and, through managerial bonuses, biasing income distribution unfairly, and at the same time ensuring that any potential cost advantage of a new zone would not be overlooked. This system, extended to all sectors, might be just the policy to reconcile short-term and long-term efficiency considerations.

It is not clear what thinking lay behind the introduction of the zonal price system in the building materials industry, although I have nowhere seen recognition of the problems mentioned here. Its most likely motivation was the desire to reduce transport costs although, as we have already seen in Chapter 4, there was not much that could be done on this score in the short term, at any rate.

We have argued that incorporation of the full differential rent into the price of the advantageously situated product may actually be inefficient from a long-term viewpoint, and that a zonal price system for raw material resources and products based upon them, with the zonal prices based principally on local production costs, may be the most efficient procedure and, furthermore, that this is the procedure that has been used at various times and in various sectors in the Soviet economy. No such fully articulated system has yet been developed for economy-wide application and, even within the building materials sector, this system neither persisted nor was consciously related to the question of economic efficiency. Nor has any theory of the economy-wide role of rent in promoting efficiency been developed. But what about rent and income?

Given the Marxian and Soviet socialist concern for distribution, it is not surprising that most Soviet discussion of differential rent has revolved around the question of income distribution and agriculture. Here the problem is similar to the problem described above of pricing resources with significantly different production cost: if national retail and wholesale prices are set for grain, say, and if farm net income is defined as gross farm revenue less materials input, farms in sections of the country with higher yields will have high earnings while their cousins in areas with lower yields will earn little, leading to sharp income inequalities. If, on the other hand, prices in any region are made to depend on actually experienced cost of production with labor input valued equally everywhere, there is no incentive to achieve the highest productivity that the land is capable of reaching. Finally, unless prices of grain can be made to reflect the production costs under optimal conditions, so that, for example, the low grain production costs in advantageously endowed areas can be reflected in prices and in land settlement patterns, efficiency in location of population is not achieved. Can the Soviet socialist system harmonize these considerations?

If these questions are not always made explicit in the Soviet discussions of pricing and attempts to measure differential advantages, they do not lie far below the surface. Experimentation over the years with differentiated procurement taxes and attempts to standardize income by extending the employee status of farmers on state farms to collective farmers are probably the two major approaches followed, but recent research has included a number of studies seeking to measure differential productivity that would permit calculation of differential rent.

What is the outlook for any of these methods? Can it be hoped to achieve total equality of income for equal work on the farms and still not encourage inefficiency? Total equality, no, but a reasonable equality and reasonable efficiency can be achieved. Any hope of perfect harmonization - total equality and efficiency - is bound to be disappointed; that perfection cannot be achieved must not be taken to mean that the system is grossly defective in these regards.

Perhaps the best evidence that efficiency and total equality cannot be achieved comes out of various recent Soviet statistical studies of agricultural productivity. The conclusions which seem to emerge are: 1) there are fairly wide variations in productivity even in small regions which would result in wide farm income variations under given regional procurement prices; 2) if procurement prices were refined further, made farm-specific, there would be little incentive to hold down costs; since any farm would be assured of covering its costs, whatever they be; but 3) since the variation within regions is significantly less than the variation between regions, that imposing a system of regional procurement prices reduces the income inequality which might otherwise result and need not stimulate inefficiency. Furthermore, setting regional procurement prices can then allow farms to vary their product mix to maximize their net income and, to the extent that local procurement price rations betray planners' preferences and goals, produce consistently with the latter. (6)

CONCLUSION

This comparative survey of the role of prices contradicts the conventional wisdom that prices perform a more useful function under capitalism than under socialism or perform it better. Problems there are, in both economies. However, we have shown that there is much room for manuever within a Marxian framework and the Soviet planners and managers have worked for many years with various pricing procedures and concepts that tend to promote rational decision making on a long-term and short-term basis. These procedures have not been fully integrated into the process of daily economic activity or been developed with the careful attention to detail that one would like to see for economy-wide rationalization. And even when modification of prices as compared with a strict cost of production view (e.g., by introducing industry wage differentials) does lead to income inequities, in the sense that some are paid more than others in relation to the onerousness of their work, the inequalities in income are rather muted, as we saw from the review of income distribution in Chapter 2. Indeed, they are extremely small in relation to what might have been expected under the continued evolution of pre-revolutionary Russia.

NOTES

(1) At the time of writing, Lange was at the University of Chicago, but he is better remembered as a Chairman of the Polish Economic Council after World War II. Perhaps the best testament to his belief that market processes need not be precluded from the operation of a socialist state, however, is the fact that Theodore O. Yntema, a co-editor along with Francis McIntyre, of Studies in Mathematical Economics in Memory of Henry Schultz (University of Chicago Press, 1942) went on to become Vice President, Finance, of the Ford Motor Company.

(2) The economic rent on capital should reflect the advantage gained by investing resources into roundabout methods of production, thus generating more tomorrow than we could consume today. This concept is usually termed the opportunity cost of capital. But interest also reflects many monetary factors which intrude on this function.

(3) In Abouchar (1977a) we also discuss these instruments from the measurement of performance over time.

(4) The extent to which wage premia reflect productivity differentials in terms of planners' priorities is discussed in the chapters by Chapman and Zielinski, 10 and 11 in Abouchar (1977a). Chapman argues that wage premia reflect priorities, although she finds little evidence for this position in a rank correlation between changes in average wages and employment in Soviet industries, while Zielinski argues that such negative evidence, together with historical ex-perience in English planning, implies that premia are not used to guide labor. On the other hand, the shifts in average wages shown by Aganbegian and Maier are striking evidence that wage premia do reflect priorities, since the key industries, such as steel and coal, are the ones that rose fastest. We hasten to observe that this need not be a conscious policy. It may well simply "have happened" under the pressure of events. As Holzman has shown, in the prewar Soviet economy the banking sector was imposing severe constraints, most notably its "real bills" policy, which in principle required that loans be made only against commercial documents such as invoices. It seems reasonable to suppose that the enforcement of this policy by the bank was weakest where the high-priority sectors were concerned, and this in turn implies that these industries would have had the greatest latitude for raising wages in their bid to attract labor, thus providing logical corroboration to the data of Aganbegian and Maier.

(5) The Standard Methodology was revised and a new version presented in 1969 ("Tipovaia metodika", 1969). A comparison of the two and assessment of the workability of the new one are contained in Abouchar (1973a.)

(6) The foregoing is best illustrated through a recent study (El'met, 1973) of land productivity in Estonia, surely a small region in the Soviet Union. In a simulation model when the farms were sown entirely with grain, the calculated net income per hectare for the different farms varied by 125 rubles; El'met's main point was that income could be made more equal, and efficiency improved by varying the cropping pattern. But this would not happen if each farm were assured a price for its grain which could cover its production costs.

8 Conclusion

In this book we have explored the main economic aspects of the performance of Soviet socialism, our interests being conditioned principally by three types of question: the adoption of the Soviet organizational framework by underdeveloped and economically developed nations, and the consistency of Soviet socialism with Marxian beliefs and concepts. We have been less concerned with questions of trade and military confrontation, although what we have said has clear bearing on these issues. That is, economic analysis is an essential ingredient for the evaluation of Soviet military capabilities, even though the latter is the subject of specialized research in its own right. Our analysis, especially that in Chapter 3, indicates that Soviet consumption remains at a low level and continues to grow slowly, probably presenting thereby a weakness from the military viewpoint since, notwithstanding the tremendous military might of the USSR which has been established independently by Western academic and intelligence sources, the capability of at the same time maintaining only low levels of consumption might suffice to deter the Soviet leadership from risking a prolonged war. However, we have also seen that, from the viewpoint of economic efficiency variously characterized, the Soviet economy is not the weak and bungling organization that it is sometimes caricatured to be, a point which the West dares miss at its own grave peril.

We have evaluated the record of Soviet socialism in terms of the economy's "executive ability," employment, inflation, income distribution, consumption, macro economic growth, and efficiency, the latter looked at within the context of spatial efficiency, efficiency in agriculture, industrial efficiency, and efficiency of the price mechanism.

Judging the economy simply in terms of its ability to get things done, the Soviet Union certainly has a solid record of performance. Although this is not very meaningful - from an economist's point of view - we must ask, not whether something gets done, but, at what cost and to what end? - frequently it is not possible to make complete evaluations. Since knowing something about this weaker criterion may be important, in the event of war, say, there is some reason to inquire into the "executive ability" of the Soviet economy. And as examples have shown time and again - the pioneering achievements and continuing performance of the Soviet space program, the development of individual industries, construction of mighty dams or railroads, the assimilation of Siberia - the economy has demonstrated great capacity in this regard, surely as great as that of a capitalist economy. Indeed, the usual move by a capitalist system to a "command economy" in time of war is possibly the best testament to this feature in the Soviet command economy.

The items just cited, of course, are not conclusive and do not constitute any indicator of the nation's overall economic welfare level, any more than the construction of pyramids, while in itself a technological achievement of the first water, reflected on the quality of life of the people of Pharaonic Egypt. Their significance is limited either to allowing us to make a prediction about the economy's ability to respond to non-economic stimuli, e.g., in wartime as noted, and also in those situations in which we must frankly acknowledge our inability to formulate a single overall economic criterion and are willing to take an engineering type of approach to the development of the economy. As we note below, such instances may be more common than professional economists are willing to admit. But first let us look at the many measures of performance which are closer to the economists' heart and about which something can be said.

We look first at employment and inflation. As we saw in Chapter 2, the annual growth rate of the Soviet economy has had its ups and downs, although the level of activity itself has almost always increased from one year to the next. While such fluctuations even in the rate of growth could present some problems for planners and could generate further instability, as a matter of fact they do not appear to have done the latter, so that one's concern is principally restricted to the question of the effect of fluctuations on employment and unemployment. And as we have noted, there have not been serious impacts on unemployment which tends to remain stable and extremely low, even when there are reductions in the economy's rate of growth. If one argues, as seems reasonable, that politicians' and economists' main concern with business fluctuations in general stems from their impact on employment, the Soviet economy certainly cannot be criticized on this ground.

When we look at inflation, we see that even in this economy which has long relied heavily on physical planning and eschewed heavy dependence upon monetary mechanisms, there has been a tremendous rate of inflation, especially during the period preceding World War II. Since consumer prices rose faster than wages, one might argue that the economy has not been able to avoid many of the ill effects of inflation. However, in the West our main concern about inflation arises on behalf of those on mixed income who are less able to adjust to the rising prices. In the Soviet Union one of the main consumption items, housing, is in extremely short supply to begin with, and is not made less accessible through inflation. Old people have traditionally lived with their families, and young people starting out have typically brought their spouses and children to live at home with the older generation. However one might lament the low level of consumption of this important consumer good, its unavailability cannot be attributed to inflation and inflation cannot be said to render life more severe for those least able to cope - the old and the young. Similarly, the fact that the prices of consumer goods rose much more rapidly than wages should not be attributed to problems in the economy's ability to manage the money supply, but should rather be taken as symptom of the fact that high-level decisions have stressed the production of producer goods rather than consumer goods. Thus, we would conclude that in general the impact of inflation has not had the same effect as in the West, where its principal impact is on people with fixed income who are generally poor to begin with.

Apparently, however, the practice which developed of using the anything-but-constant 26/27 prices to evaluate enterprise performance in the rapid pre-war inflation (i.e., using unadjusted prices for old products and heavily inflated current prices for new products) did take its toll by exacerbating the rate of product turnover. Income distribution (wage and salary income), we saw, is substantially more equal than in Western industrially developed economies, and vastly more equal than in most developing countries, although it does not achieve the goal of complete equality that some might associate with Marx. Taking property and income taxes into consideration renders the Soviet income distribution relatively still more equal than that in industrial-ized capitalist economies; making allowance also for the relatively higher prices of non-basic consumption in the Soviet Union makes that country's distribution of consumption, which is what we are ultimately concerned about, more equal yet.

The Soviet growth record, especially during its takeoff into industrialization in the 1930s has been striking indeed. As the most appropriate measure of the ability of the economy to grow, we chose that rate which is calculated as the average over a series of sub-periods, in each sub-period the growth being calculated in terms of end-year weighted prices in conformity with Bergson-Moorsteen theory. For this we found a growth rate which is among the highest experienced by economies which have industrialized since the mid-1800s or earlier. The Soviet "century" coefficient, the number of times that a country would grow during a one hundred-year period - assuming its annual growth rate over the entire period was equal to that over some shorter base line - when based on a long forty-seven-year period of observation, was from ten to forty times as great as that found for twelve other countries by Simon Kuznets. Its century coefficient based on a short 1950-62 period exceeds the century coefficient of all but two of the eleven countries in Edward Denison's study of postwar growth. This should be tempered by the recognition, as we have noted several times, that growth of consumption, which is the ultimate payoff for people, has been much slower.

Growth is nice, but efficiency is better, better at least from the viewpoint of a nation which is considering embarking on one course or another. Is a country developing as efficiently as it can, and can this efficiency be taken as a reflection of the particular economic system, or is its growth rather a reflection of the historical social traditions of its people? Is it maximizing the rate of growth, and over how long a period can it continue to do so? Or is it growing wastefully? Is it squandering either resources or a large portion of current output? In all these questions we are interested in distinguishing between, on the one hand, the resource endowment of the economy and the peculiar traditions of the people, which may have some bearing on efficiency, and, on the other hand, the system itself.

We pointed out the many obstacles to the investigation of efficiency. But we believe that enough has been shown to dispel the widely held notion that the Soviet Union is inefficient. We showed that transportation, which many Soviet writers themselves have believed to be inefficient, has not been. During the 1930s there was some inefficiency in location. There were also some compromises with spatial efficiency which took the form of disproportionate allocation of investment to regions with somewhat lower productivity, apparently in an attempt to break down secessionist elements, as in Ukraine. These do not appear to have been too costly, however, and in view of the political constraints as perceived by Moscow were probably excusable.

The unambiguously inefficient location pattern that we did discover was in the cement industry where, in fact, a total social cost minimizing location pattern should have been an easy matter and, indeed, investigation of the cement industry after World War II showed that the prewar inefficient location patterns were later corrected. We conclude that spatial inefficiency is not an integral concomitant of Soviet socialist development. Similarly, in agriculture we showed that there may be some types of inefficiency, but there is some reason to believe that much of it is due to low levels of skill acquisition and schooling, resulting in turn from the leadership's preference for industrial development. Egregious forms of inefficiency that may be observed in agriculture - and there have been some - are traceable to the concentration of untrammeled power in the hands of a supreme agricultural ruler whose decisions might be capricious. This weakness does certainly reflect on the system and is, furthermore, a weakness which it would be difficult to preclude in any economy, especially when the prime minister himself virtually becomes the agricultural tsar, as was the case with Khrushchev.

Inefficiency in industry, we argued, is not as dramatic or as extensive as many writers believe. Many of the behavioral expectations of managers may either be unfounded, or else may after all prove not to have the consequences anticipated. Our own study of one important industry, hydraulic cement production, in which there have been large advances since World War II in productivity and extensive experimentation with an adoption of new technology, demonstrates this thesis.

Finally, recognizing the great difficulty in trying to comment on the degree of efficiency of an industry, sector, or economy, we attempted to analyze the decision rules of the economy or, at least, one basic component of decision rules - the price mechanism. We saw that the price mechanism in the Western capitalist world is far from perfect as a transmitter of signals and to attain efficiency. It is also imperfect in the Soviet Union but there is nothing that dooms it to be so, no reason why as time progresses there cannot be modification and improvement of price relationships to promote more efficient decision making. Our analysis of the alleged Marxian obstacles to rational price formulation, as well as our comparative discussion of the possible inconsistencies that may exist between different functions of prices, which recognizes more explicitly than is customarily done the contradictions and inconsistencies in capitalist price systems, shows both the tremendous challenge involved in developing a harmonious price mechanism and the flexibility which the economy's managers have at their disposal.

But it has been our intention to analyze these aspects of Soviet socialism with a finer glass, considering each of them from one of the major viewpoints of interest to us, as stated at the outset of this chapter. This analysis is summarized in Table 8.1. In the column headings we indicate the main aspects of interest and, in the row stub, the viewpoint of interest. Each square then indicates the nature of the relationship between a particular aspect of the economy's performance and the viewpoint of concern.

The table is self-explanatory and suggests certain conclusions. First, the development and organization of the Soviet economy are consistent with Marx's thought and objectives. The Soviet Union has occasionally been faulted on even this score - by some Westerners critical of the degree of income inequality observed there and by some communist cousins, such as Yugoslavia, which maintains that it alone is a Marxian socialist state, with the USSR being merely a variant of capitalism in which the state is the main proprietor of capital. As we have seen, there is income inequality, but it is much more limited than in the West, especially when non-wage and salary income is taken into account, and even more limited, relatively, if income in kind is added. Moreover, as noted in Chapter 2, income inequality is much narrower than in countries such as Brazil, which undoubtedly provides a better indication of the economic and social development that Tsarist Russia might have followed in the absence of a revolution.

From the viewpoint of industrialized economies contemplating a change of organization, which increasingly appears a possibility in Western Europe where local communist parties are developing greater power, it would appear that, on the basis of the evidence presented in this book and summarized in Table 8.1, there would be no great advantage in adopting a Soviet type of organizational structure. There would undoubtedly be some narrowing of differentials in personal income; a dictatorial state might eliminate certain deadweight losses such as those which accompany frequent labor stoppages, as well as those arising in economic cycles which could probably be muted; employment and unemployment patterns would stabilize, possibly even reducing unemployment levels to pure frictional unemployment consisting only of job changers. However, all these together would not represent a major achievement as compared with the present state of

TABLE 8.1. Nature of Relationship between Aspects of Soviet Performance and Sources of Interest in Soviet Socialism

Source of Interest	Aspect of Performance			
	Economic Growth	Economic Efficiency	Income Distribution	Other
Consistency with Marxian tenents	Little relevance to Marx's views	Attainment of economic efficiency not inconsistent with Marx. In practice, although efficiency not fully achieved, certainly not precluded by subscription to Marx (e.g., price efficiency not precluded)	Income distribution consistent with Marx and Marxist goals of achieving greater share for proletariat (and small farmers)	Although fluctuations in annual performance not eliminated, no involuntary unemployment in economy
Adoption of Soviet-type organization by industrially developed capitalist economy	Record of post WWII growth among leading performances in world but by no means unique (c.f. Japan, Germany, France, Italy)	Soviet efficiency comparable to that in Western industrialized capitalist nations	Distribution of wage and salary income narrower; distribution of total income (including non-wage and salary and public sector goods and services) much more equal in Soviet Union than in Western industrialized capitalist nations.	As above
Adoption of Soviet development model and/or organization by Third World countries	Growth much better than Third World countries under capitalism	Much more efficient than Third World countries	Much narrower income distribution than exists in most Third World countries (excluding those with very low income levels where all people are poor); also, much narrower distribution than would probably have developed under Tsarist evolution	As above; also note high level of public sector services (e.g., health and education)

133

such economies and they would, moreover, be bought at great sacrifice of personal freedoms. The point is that while Soviet socialism enabled the country to emerge from backwardness and achieve a very high rate of growth, with a century coefficient whether extrapolated on the basis of short or long periods of observation outstripping that of almost every industrialized nation today, its recent rate of growth is comparable to that of most of the latter nations. Indeed, while the differences may not be ascribable simply to statistical error in the technical sense, given the indeterminateness of the welfare-GNP relationship, we should be careful not to place too great stress on differences of a point or so in the annual growth rates which are now being observed. Thus, it would appear that there is little to gain in terms of growth by restructuring a Western industrialized economy along lines of Soviet socialism.

Viewed from the standpoint of Third World countries, however, Soviet performance is much more compelling. The Soviet growth record, especially its breaking out of the straits of Tsarist economic backwardness, has surpassed the growth of any twentieth-century developing country, most of which are based more or less on private ownership of the means of production. Accompanied as Soviet growth has been by the attainment of reasonable equity in income distribution, its income distribution being several orders of magnitude more equal than that in all except the poorest developing countries in which almost everyone is reduced to the poorest common denominator, it holds out great promise on this score as well. Thus, the obvious cases of successful development under private ownership, Taiwan, Zaire, and South Korea, for example, are marked by sharp income inequalities. These inequalities are frequently exacerbated by venality and corruption on the part of the political administration, in sharp contrast with the situation in many of the highly disciplined socialist economies, especially the Soviet Union.

To be sure, any comment on the relationship between economic development and income equality, on the one hand, and organizational form, on the other, must also take account of cases of genuine or nominal socialism which are accompanied by failure. But it is very hard to discover cases of failure of countries genuinely commited to socialism; certainly there are no such failures in economies like the Soviet Union. Some economies which are only nominally committed to socialism - Egypt being the most prominent here - have not been successful so far, although the lack of success is ascribable more to the lack of economic discipline in Egypt as contrasted with the more genuinely socialist economies. Finally, there have been other recent examples of successful development with socialism starting from a low base. Most notable here is Iraq's performance during the sixties (i.e., even before the big jump in oil prices) where the 3% annual population growth did not prevent a per capita growth in GNP of 3% or greater (total growth exceeding 6% per annum), and where fair equity was achieved in the distribution of the nation's consumption. In this achievement, Iraq placed less stress on intense industrial growth and more on agriculture than did the Soviet Union, choosing not to adhere so determinedly to a policy of industrial self-sufficiency. Undoubtedly

Iraq, a small country, could afford the luxury of more balanced growth by virtue of being a late-comer, with countries in both camps already existing so that it could trade with both without fear of economic domination by either. This policy, however, suggests that even adopting the main organizational and structural characteristics of Soviet socialism does not require complete emulation of Soviet policies to achieve a comparable record.

Finally, we observe that the political institutions in many Third World capitalist countries today are not noticeably more enlightened than the Soviet political system. For such countries to adopt an organizational framework similar to that of Soviet socialism, therefore, does not imply as great political compromise as might be the case in many industrially advanced economies. Unless such economies are able to institute greater political liberalism, not to speak of greater economic progress, Soviet socialism does and will increasingly represent a more attractive model.

Bibliography

Abouchar, Alan. "The Consistency and Efficiency of Interest and Economic Rent." In Abouchar, ed. The Socialist Price Mechanism. Durham, N.C.: Duke University Press, 1977.

Abouchar, Alan. "An Economic Analysis of the Hall Commission Report." Toronto: Ontario Economic Council Discussion Paper Series, 1977.

Abouchar, Alan. "Indexing Inflation: Lessons from Brazil." Canadian Forum, August 1975.

Abouchar, Alan. "A New Approach to the Evaluation and Construction of Highway User Charges." Eastern Economic Journal, July 1974.

Abouchar, Alan. "The New Soviet Standard Methodology for Investment Allocation." Soviet Studies, January 1973.

Abouchar, Alan. "Postwar Developments in the Soviet Cement Industry." In U.S. Congress, JEC, Soviet Economy in a New Perspective. Washington, D.C.: U.S. G.P.O., 1976.

Abouchar, Alan. "Les primes de salaire comme succedane d'interest en Union Sovietique." Revue de l'Est, April 1973.

Abouchar, Alan, ed. The Socialist Price Mechanism. Durham, N.C.: Duke University Press, 1977.

Abouchar, Alan. Soviet Planning and Spatial Efficiency. Bloomington: Indiana University Press, 1971.

Abouchar, Alan. Transportation Economics and Public Policy. New York: Wiley-Interscience, 1977.

Abouchar, Alan and Needles, Daniel. "Custom Combining: A Neglected Opportunity for Soviet Agriculture." Canadian Slavonic Papers, March 1975.

Aganbegian, A.G. and Maier, V.F. Zarabotnaia plata v SSSR [Wages in the USSR] . Moscow: Gosplanizdat, 1959.

Ahluwalia, Montek. "Income Inequality: Some Dimensions of the Problem." In Chenery, et al., eds., Redistribution with Growth. London: Oxford University Press, 1974.

American Association of State Highway Officials (AASHO). The AASHO Road Test: Proceedings of a Conference held May 16-18, 1962, St. Louis, Mo., Highway Research Board Special Report no. 73. National Academy of Science, Washington, D.C., 1962.

American Society for Testing and Materials. ASTM Standards on Cement. September 1958.

Arnold, Arthur Z. Banks, Credit, and Money in Soviet Russia. New York: Columbia University Press, 1937.

Astanskii, L. Iu. and Liusov, A.N. "Polnoe osyoenie moshcnosteiosnova uvelicheniia proizvodstva, tsementa" ["Complete Utilization of Capacity is the Basis for Raising Production"] . Tsement, no. 4, 1965.

Baer, Werner and Kerstenezky, Issac. Inflation and Growth in Latin America. Homewood, Ill.: Richard D. Irwin, 1964.

Basic Directions. "Osnovnye napravleniia razvitiia nar. khoz. SSSR na 1976-1980 gody" ["Basic Directions for the Development of the National Economy of the USSR, 1976-1980"] . Ekonomicheskaia gazeta, no. 11, March 1976.

Becker, Abraham. Soviet National Income, 1958-1964. Berkeley and Los Angeles: University of California Press, 1969.

Belov, G.G.   "K voprosu ob optimal'noi moshchnosti tsementnykh zavodv" ["The Question of the Optimal Capacity of Cement Plants"] . Tsement, no. 6, 1955.

Bergson, Abram. The Economics of Soviet Planning. New Haven and London: Yale University Press, 1964.

Bergson, Abram. The Real National Income of Soviet Russia Since 1928. Cambridge: Harvard University Press, 1961.

Bergson, Abram, ed. Soviet Economic Growth. Evanston, Ill." Row, Peterson, 1953.

Berliner, Joseph. "Flexible Pricing and New Products in the USSR." Soviet Studies 28, no. 4, October 1975.

Berliner, Joseph. Factory and Manager in the USSR. Cambridge: Harvard University Press, 1968.

Bol'shaia sovetskaia entsiklopediia [The Great Soviet Encyclopedia] . Vol. 8, referred to as BSE, 1970.

Bornstein, Morris. "Soviet Price Theory and Policy." In New Directions in the Soviet Economy, part I. U.S. Congress, JEC. Washington, D.C.: U.S. G.P.O., 1966.

Brodskii, G. "Geografiia potrebleniia tsementa v SSSR" ["The Geography of Cement Consumption"]. Tsement, no. 6, 1938.

Brodskii, G. "Perspektivy razvitiia tsementnoi promyshlennosti v tretei piatiletke" ["Prospects for the Development of the Cement Industry During the Third Five-Year Plan"]. Nashe stroitel'stvo [Our Construction], no. 23, 1937.

Brodskii, G. "Sekratit' radius destavki tsementa" ["Reduce the Length of Cement Shipments"]. Tsement, no. 5/6, 1937.

Brodskii, G. "Vazhneishaia zadacha tsementnoi promyshlennosti" ["The Most Important Task for the Cement Industry"]. Nashe stroitel' stvo [Our Construction], 1935.

Bronson, David W. "Scientific and Engineering Manpower in the USSR and Employment in R & D." In U.S. Congress, JEC. Washington, D.C.: U.S. G.P.O., 1973.

Brown, Emily Clark. Soviet Trade Unions and Labor Relations. Cambridge: Harvard University Press, 1965.

Budnikov, P.P. and Volkonskii, B.V. "The Most Universal and Widespread Building Material." Tsement, no. 5, 1967.

Campbell, Robert W. The Economics of Soviet Oil and Gas. Baltimore: Johns Hopkins University Press, 1967.

Carey, David W. "Developments in Soviet Education." In U.S. Congress, JEC. Washington, D.C.: U.S. G.P.O., 1973.

Cembureau. Cement Standards of the World. Paris: The European Cement Association, 1968.

Chapman, Janet. "Soviet Wages Under Socialism." In Abouchar, ed., Socialist Price Mechanism. Durham, N.C.: Duke University Press, 1977.

Chapman, Janet. Real Wages in Soviet Russia Since 1928. Cambridge: Harvard University Press, 1963.

Chenery, Hollis; Ahluwalia, Montek S.; Bell, C.L.G.; Duloy, John H.; and Jolly, Richard. Redistribution with Growth. London: Oxford University Press, 1974.

Clark, M. Gardner. The Economics of Soviet Steel. Cambridge: Harvard University Press, 1955.

Conklin, D.W. "Barriers to Technological Change in the USSR: A Study of Chemical Fertilizers." Soviet Studies, January 1969.

"Constitution of the USSR." Pravda, October 8, 1977.

Denison, Edward F. Why Growth Rates Differ: Postwar Experience in Nine Western Countries. Washington, D.C.": The Brookings Institute, 1967.

Dobb, Maurice. Soviet Economic Development Since 1917. New York: International Publishers, 1948.

El'met, Kh. A. "K voprosu o razmeshchenii sel'skokhoziaistvennykh kultur" ["On the Location of Agricultural Crops"]. Ekon mat. met, vol. 9, no. 4, 1973. English translation in Matekon 11, no. 1, 1974.

Erlich, Alexander. The Soviet Industrialization Debate, 1924-1928. Cambridge: Harvard University Press, 1960.

Evodokimenko, A. "Sebestoimost', tsena, effektivinost'" ["Prime Cost, Price, Effectiveness"]. Ekonomicheskaia gazeta, February 3, 1965.

Fallenbuchl, Zbigniew M. Economic Development in the Soviet Union and Eastern Europe, vol. 2. New York: Praeger, 1976.

Fishlow, Albert. "Brazilian Size Distribution of Income." American Economic Review, May 1972.

Gershenkron, Alexander. A Dollar Index of Soviet Machinery Output, 1927-28 to 1937. Santa Monica: The Rand Corporation, 1951.

Greenslade, Rush. "Industrial Production Statistics in the USSR." In Treml and Hardt, eds., Soviet Economic Statistics. Durham, N.C.: Duke University Press, 1972.

Greenslade, Rush. The Real Gross National Product of the USSR 1950-1975. In U.S. Congress, JEC. Washington, D.C.: U.S. G.P.O., 1976.

Grokhotov, N.V. and Kroptov, V.A. "Ispol' zovanie otkhodov drugikh otraslei promyshlennosti" ["The Use of Wastes from Other Industries"]. Tsement, no. 5, 1963.

Grossman, Gregory. "Price Control, Incentives, and Innovation in the Soviet Economy." In Abouchar, ed., The Socialist Price Mechanism. Durham, N.C.: Duke University Press, 1977.

Grossman, Gregory. "National Income." In Bergson, ed., Soviet Economic Growth. Evanston, Ill.: Row, Peterson, 1953.

Grude, E.N. "Model' optimizassi proizvodstvennoi struktury sel'skokhoziaisvennogo predpriatiia" [A Model for Optimizing the Production Structure of the Agricultural Enterprise"]. Ekonomika i matematicheskie metody, no. 5, 1975.

Gudkov, L.V.; Kuznetsov, B.B.; Mikhailov, V.V.; and Nezhintsev, G.E. "Razmeshchenie tsementnykh zavodov s uchetom vida teklnologicheskogo topliva" ["The Location of Cement Plants Taking Account of the Technological Fuel Type"] . Tsement, no. 10, 1969.

Gutsev, E.G. "Perevozka mineral'nyka stroitel' nykh materialov" ["The Shipment of Mineral Building Materials"]. Chapter II in Gutsev, et al., Ratsionalizatsiia perevozok massovykh gruzov v BSSR, Minsk, 1960.

Gutsev, E.G. et al. Ratsionalizatsiia perevosok massovykh v BSSR [Rationalization of Mass Freight Shipments in the Belorussian SSR] . Minsk: Izdatel'stvo Akademii Nauk BSSR, 1960.

Hodgman, Donald. Soviet Industrial Production, 1928-1951. Cambridge: Harvard University Press, 1964.

Holzman, Franklyn D. "The Ural Kuznetsk Combine: A Study in Investment Criteria." Quarterly Journal of Economics, May 1962.

Holzman, Franklyn D. "Soviet Inflationary Pressures, 1928-1957: Causes and Cures." Quarterly Journal of Economics 74, no. 2, May 1960.

Hutchings, Raymond. "Fluctuations in Soviet Industrial Growth Rates." Soviet Studies, January 1969.

Hunter, Holland. Soviet Transportation Policy. Cambridge: Harvard University Press, 1957.

Il'in, I. and Vezlomtsev, V.I. "Planirovat' proizvodztvo i potreblenie tsementa s uchemtom ego kachestvo" ["Plan Cement Production and Consumption with Regard for its Quality"] . Tsement, no. 5, 1963.

Jasny, Naum. "Production Costs and Prices in Soviet Agriculture." In Karcz, ed., Soviet and East European Agriculture. Berkley and Los Angeles: University of California, 1967.

Jasny, Naum. Khrushchev's Crop Policies. Glasgow: Outram, 1964.

Jasny, Naum. Soviet Industrialization, 1928-1952. Chicago: Chicago University Press, 1961.

Jasny, Naum. "Prospects for Soviet Farm Output and Labor." Review of Economics and Statistics, May 1954.

Jasny, Naum. The Soviet Economy During the Plan Era. Palo Alto: Stanford University Press (Food Research Institute), 1951.

Jasny, Naum. The Socialized Agriculture of the USSR. Palo Alto: Stanford University Press, 1949.

Johnson, D. Gale. "The Soviet Livestock Sector: Problems and Prospects." The ACES Bulletin, vol. 16, no. 2, Fall 1974.

Joravsky, David. "Ideology and Progress in Crop Rotation." In Karcz, ed., Soviet and East European Agriculture. Berkeley and Los Angeles: University of California, 1967.

Kahan, Arcadius. "The Problems of the 'Agrarian-Industrial' Complexes in the Soviet Union." In Fallenbuchl, Economic Development in the Soviet Union and Eastern Europe, vol. 2. New York: Praeger, 1976.

Kaplan, Norman. "Growth in Soviet Transportation and Communications." American Economic Review 62, no. 5, December 1967.

Kaplan, Norman and Moorsteen, Richard. "An Index of Soviet Industrial Output." American Economic Review 50, June 1960.

Kapustin, E.I. Kachestvo truda i zarabotnaia plata [Labor Quality and Wages] . Moscow: "Mysl'," 1964.

Karcz, Jerry. ed. Soviet and East European Agriculture. Berkeley and Los Angeles: University of California, 1967.

Katz, Zev. "Insights from Emigres and Sociological Studies on the Soviet Union." In U.S. Congress, JEC. Washington, D.C.: U.S. G.P.O., 1973.

Kirsch, Leonard J. Soviet Wages: Changes in Structure and Administration Since 1956. Cambridge: MIT Press, 1972.

Kobrin, M.G. and Liusov, A.N. "Puti snizheniia izderzhek na tsement v sfere obrashcheniia" ["Ways to Reduce Cement Costs in the Distribution Sphere"]. Tsement, no. 10, 1969.

Koropeckyj, I.S. Location Problems in the Soviet Industry Before World War II: The Case of the Ukraine. Chapel Hill, N.C.: University of North Carolina Press, 1971.

Kostin, Leonid. Wages in the USSR. Moscow: Foreign Languages Publishing House, 1960.

Kosygin, A.N. Address to the 25th Party Congress. Ekonomicheskaia gazeta, no. 10, March 1976.

Kravchenko, I.V.; Entin, Z.B.; and Oleinikova, N.I. "O sovershen-stvovanii deistvuiushchikh standartov na tsementy" ["Improving the Existing Standards for Cement"]. Tsement, no. 11, 1969.

Kuznets, Simon. Modern Economic Growth: Rate, Structure and Spread. New Haven: Yale University Press, 1966.

Lange, Oskar. "On the Economic Theory of Socialism." From Lange and Frederick Taylor, On the Economic Theory of Socialism. Minneapolis: University of Minneapolis Press, 1938. Lange's article was first published in slightly different form in Review of Economic Studies, 1936-7 and was reprinted in Alec Nove and D.M. Nuti, eds., Socialist Economics, Baltimore, Md.: Penguin Books, 1972.

Lange, Oskar; McIntyre, Francis; and Yntema, Theodore O. Studies in Mathematical Economics in Memory of Henry Schultz. Chicago: University of Chicago Press, 1942.

Liusov, A.N. "Ekonomika tsementoi promyshlennosti" ["The Economics of the Cement Industry"]. Tsement, no. 4, 1970.

Liusov, A.N. "O spetsializatsii tsementnykh zavodov" ["On the Specialization of Cement Plants"]. Tsement, no. 6, 1963.

Loginov, Z.I. Tsementnaia promyshlennost SSSR [The Cement Industry of the USSR]. Moscow: Gosplanizat, 1959.

Loginov, Z.I. Razmeshchenie proizvodstva i perevozki tsementa [Location of Production and the Shipment of Cement]. Moscow: Promstroiizdat, 1957.

Loginov, Z.I. "Ob optimal'noi moshchnosti tsementnykh zavodov" ["On the Optimal Capacity of Cement Plants"]. Tsement, no. 4, 1955.

Lur'e, Iu. S. Portlandtsement [Portland Cement]. Leningrad: Gosstroiizdat, 1959 and 1964.

Machlup, Fritz. The Basing-Point System. Philadelphia: Blakiston, 1949.

Marx, Karl. Critique of the Gotha Programme. C.P. Dutt, ed. New York: International Publishers, 1938.

Medvedev, Zh. The Rise and Fall of T.D. Lysenko. Translated with an introduction by I. Michael Lerner. New York: Columbia University Press, 1969.

Moorsteen, Richard. "On Measuring Potential and Relative Efficiency." Quarterly Journal of Economics, August 1961.

Moorsteen, Richard and Powell, Raymond. The Soviet Capital Stock, 1928-1962. Homewood, Ill.: Irwin, 1966.

Moroz, I.K. "Povyshenie kachestva tsementa glavnaia zadacha" ["Raising Cement Quality is an Important Task"] . Tsement, no. 1, 1965.

Musgrave, Richard. The Theory of Public Finance. New York: McGraw-Hill, 1959.

Narkhoz. Naradnoe khoziaistrvo SSSR. Moscow: "Statisika," various years.

Nash, Edmund. "Recent Changes in Labor Controls in the Soviet Union." In U.S. Congress, JEC. Part III, The Human Resources. Washington, D.C.: U.S. G.P.O., 1966.

Nash, Edmund. "Purchasing Power of Workers in the USSR." The Monthly Labor Review, April 1960.

NKPS. Materialy po statistike putei soobshcheniia, Vyp. 108, Svodnaia statistika perevozok po sheleznym dorogam za 1927/28 operats. god, Tom II [Statistics on Means of Communications, no. 108, Summary Statistics of Railway Freight for the Fiscal Year 1927/28, vol. 2]. Moscow: Transpechat', 1930.

Noren, James. "Soviet Industry Trends in Output, Inputs, and Productivity." U.S. Congress, JEC. Washington, D.C.: U.S. G.P.O., 1966.

Nove, Alec. "Agricultural Performance Compared: Belorussia and Eastern Poland." In Fallenbuchl, Economic Development in the Soviet Union and Eastern Europe, vol. 2. New York: Praeger, 1976.

Nove, Alec. "Will Russia Ever Feed Itself?" N.Y. Times Magazine, February 1, 1976.

Nove, Alec. "Was Stalin Really Necessary?" Encounter, April 1962.

Nove, Alec. "The Problem of 'Success Indicators' in Soviet Industry." Economica, NS 25, no. 97, February 1958.

Nove, Alec. "1926/27 and All That." Soviet Studies, October 1957.

Nove, Alec and Laird, Roy. "A Note on Labour Utilization in the Kolkhoz." Soviet Studies, April 1953.

Nutter, Warren. The Growth of Industrial Production in the Soviet Union. New York: National Bureau of Economic Research, Princeton University Press, 1962.

Petrakov, N. Ia. "K probleme soizmereniia zatrat i rezul'tatov" ["On the Problem of Comparing Costs and Results"]. Ekon i mat. met., 10, no. 4, 1974.

Pomiluiko, V.I. "Novoe v pasportizatsii tsementa" ["What's New in Cement Specifications"]. Tsement, no. 2, 1954.

Pospielovsky, Dmitri. "The 'Link System' in Soviet Agriculture." Soviet Studies, April 1970.

Promyshlennost' SSSR, 1964.

Promyshlennost' 1957. Tssu, Promyshlennost' SSSR, Statisticheskii sbornik [Industry of the USSR - a Statistical Compendium]. Moscow: Gosstatizat, 1957.

Rabkina, N.E. and Rimashevskaia, N.M. Osnovy differentsiatsii zarabotnoi platy i dokhodov naseleniia [The Principles of Wage and Income Differentiation]. Moscow: "Ekonomika," 1972.

Schinke, Eberhard. "Soviet Agricultural Statistics." In Treml and Hardt, eds., Soviet Economic Statistics. Durham, N.C.: Duke University Press, 1972.

Seton, Francis. "The Question of Ideological Obstacles to Rational Price Setting in Communist Countries." In Abouchar, ed., Socialist Price Mechanism. Durham, N.C.: Duke University Press, 1977.

Seton, Francis. "The Tempo of Soviet Industrial Expansion." Bulletin of the Oxford University Institute of Statistics, vol. 20, February 1958.

Shatalov, E.S. "Zadachi tsementnoi promyshlennosti" ["Tasks of the Cement Industry"]. Ts., no. 4, 1938.

Shimkin, Dmitri and Leedy, Richard. "Soviet Industrial Growth." Automotive Industries, no. 1, 1958.

Shneider, V. and Brodskii, G. "Itogi i perspektivy razmeshcheniia tsementnoi promyshlennosti" ["Performance and Prospect in Locating the Cement Industry"]. PKh, no. 2, 1939.

Shroeder, Gertrude and Severin, Barbara S. "Soviet Consumption and Income Policies in Perspective." In U.S. Congress, JEC. Washington, D.C.: U.S. G.P.O., 1976.

Smekov, M.M. "Proizvoditel'nost' truda - eto samoe glavnoe" ["Labor Productivity is the Most Important Job"]. Tsement, no. 4, 1970.

Smith, Hedrick. The Russians. New York: Quadrangle Books, 1975.

Spravochnik po proizvodstvu tsementa [Cement Production Hand-book]. Gosstroiizdat, 1963.

"Standarty razlichnykh stran na portland tsement" ["Portland Cement Standards of Different Countries"] . Tsement, no. 5, 1959.

Smurov, A. and Slivitskii, S. "O perevozkakh tsementa" ["Cement Shipments"]. Tsement, no. 7, 1936.

Stuart, Robert. The Collective Farm in Soviet Agriculture. Lexington, Mass.: Heath, 1972.

Thornton, Judith. "Value-Added and Factor Productivity in Soviet Industry." American Economic Review, December 1970.

Thornton, Judith. "Discussion" [of Joseph Berliner, "The Static Efficiency of the Soviet Economy"]. American Economic Review, May 1964.

"Tipovaia metodika opredeleniia ekonomicheskoi kapital'nykh vlozhenii." Ekonomicheskaia gazeta [The Economic Gazette], no. 39. Trans-lated as "Standard Methodology for Determining Effectiveness of Capital Investments." Matekon 8, no. 1, 1970.

"Tipovaia metodika opredeleniia ekonomicheskoi effektivnosti kapital'nykh vlozhenii i novoi tekniki v narodnom khoziaistve SSSR 1960" ["Standard Methodology for Determining the Economic Effectiveness of Capital Investments in New Equipment in the National Economy of the USSR"]. Planovoe khoziaistvo [The Planned Economy], no. 3.

Toda, Yasushi. "An International Comparison of Urban Consumption: Russia and the United States before World War I." Keisai Kenkyu 22, no. 1, January 1971.

Treml, Vladimir G. and Hardt, John P., eds. Soviet Economic Statistics. Durham, N.C.: Duke University Press, 1972.

Tsement [Cement]. Advertisement on back cover. No. 4, 1966.

Tssu. (Central Statistical Administration). Promyshlennost' 1964, Statisticheskii sbornik [Industry in 1964, A Statistical Handbook]. Moscow: "Statistika," 1964.

"Uluchshat' kachestvo tsementa" ["Improve Product Quality"] . Tse-ment, no. 4, 1964.

U.S. Bureau of Mines, Department of the Interior. Minerals Yearbook, vol. I-II. Washington, D.C., 1968.

U.S. Congress, Joint Economic Committee (JEC). Soviet Economy in a New Perspective. Washington, D.C.: U.S. G.P.O., 1976.

U.S. Congress, Joint Economic Committee (JEC). Soviet Economic Prospects for the Seventies. Washington, D.C.: U.S. G.P.O., 1973.

U.S. Congress, Joint Economic Committee (JEC), 1966. New Directions in the Soviet Economy. Washington, D.C.: U.S. G.P.O., 1966.

Vezlomtsev, V.I.   "Sovershenstvovat' metody alaliza effektivnosti
    proizvodstva" ["Improve Methods to Analyze the Effectiveness of
    Production"] . Tsement, no. 3, 1966.

Volkonskii, B.V. and Shteiert, N.P.   "Rol' standartov v povyshenii
    kachestva tsementa" ["The Role of Standards in the Improvement
    of Cement Quality"] . Tsement, no. 3, 1965.

Whitehouse, Douglas and Havelka, Joseph F.   "Comparison of Farm
    Output in the U.S. and USSR, 1950-1971." In U.S. Congress, JEC.
    Washington, D.C.: U.S. G.P.O., 1973.

Wiles, Peter and Markowski, Stefan.   "Income Distribution Under
    Communism." Soviet Studies, January 1971.

Yezhov, A.I.   Statistika premyshlennosti   [Statistics of Industry] .
    Moscow: "Statistika," 1965.

Zakharova, N.   "Opyr raboty tsementnykh zavodov na gazoobraznom
    topliv" ["The Experience of Cement Plants Working with Gaseous
    Fuels"] . Tsement, no. 6, 1959.

Zielinski, Janusz G.   "Soviet Wages: Comments and Extensions." In
    Abouchar, ed., Socialist Price Mechanism.   Durham, N.C.:   Duke
    University Press, 1977.

Index

About the Author

ALAN ABOUCHAR is Professor of Economics at the University of Toronto. His research, dealing primarily with the Soviet economy, transportation economics and planning, and urban economic analysis, has taken the form of books (Transportation Economics and Public Policy, The Socialist Price Mechanism (ed.), Soviet Planning and Spatial Efficiency) and articles in leading professional journals and collections. Professor Abouchar has served as consultant to public sector agencies in Brazil, Canada, Iraq, Ontario, Yugoslavia, and West Africa in the fields of transportation, urban planning, and regional economics. He was, for nine years, editor of Matekon and is currently editor of the Eastern Economic Journal. His academic degrees include Ph.D. (economics) and M.A. (statistics) from the University of California at Berkeley, A.M. and B.A. degrees (economics) from New York University, and M.A. (pure mathematics) from York University.

Pergamon Policy Studies